"Self-care is serious, especially in the helping professions. Packed full of psychological wisdom and anchored in Scripture, this work is a lifeline for those who are exhausted, empty, and need to bring balance back into their lives."

Dr. Tim Clinton, president, American Association of Christian Counselors

"If you or someone you love is burning out, Jonathan Hoover's book will help tremendously. *Stress Fracture* is your go-to guide for getting your life back and enjoying it."

Georgia Shaffer, PA licensed psychologist, professional certified coach (PCC), and author of *Taking Out Your Emotional Trash*

"*Stress Fracture* delivers profound wisdom from a biblical perspective. Offering holistic strategies, it empowers readers to overcome burnout physically, relationally, spiritually, occupationally, and navigationally. This is a vital resource in encouraging anyone through seasons of burnout!"

Dr. Benny Tate, pastor of Rock Springs Church and author of *Defy the Odds* and *Unlimited*

"In *Stress Fracture*, Jonathan Hoover, PhD, offers a comprehensive and insightful guide to overcoming burnout and ways to reclaim your well-being. Hoover provides practical strategies to help readers navigate life's challenges and build resilience. This book is a must-read for anyone struggling with burnout or seeking to prevent it in the future."

Dr. Wayne Cordeiro, New Hope Church & College and author of *Leading on Empty*

STRESS FRACTURE

STRESS FRACTURE

YOUR ULTIMATE GUIDE TO BEATING BURNOUT

JONATHAN HOOVER, PhD

BETHANYHOUSE
a division of Baker Publishing Group
Minneapolis, Minnesota

© 2024 by Jonathan Hoover

Published by Bethany House Publishers
Minneapolis, Minnesota
BethanyHouse.com

Bethany House Publishers is a division of
Baker Publishing Group, Grand Rapids, Michigan

Printed in the United States of America

Library of Congress Cataloging-in-Publication Data
Names: Hoover, Jonathan, author.
Title: Stress fracture : your ultimate guide to beating burnout / Jonathan Hoover.
Description: Minneapolis, Minnesota : Bethany House Publishers, a division of Baker Publishing Group, [2024] | Includes bibliographical references.
Identifiers: LCCN 2023053580 | ISBN 9780764243424 (paper) | ISBN 9780764243929 (casebound) | ISBN 9781493448029 (ebook)
Subjects: LCSH: Burn out (Psychology) | Job stress. | Stress (Psychology)
Classification: LCC BF481 .H64 2024 | DDC 158.7/23—dc23/eng/20240304
LC record available at https://lccn.loc.gov/2023053580

Cover design by T J Nix

Published in association with Books & Such Literary Management, www.books andsuch.com.

Baker Publishing Group publications use paper produced from sustainable forestry practices and postconsumer waste whenever possible.

24 25 26 27 28 29 30   7 6 5 4 3 2 1

For my dad

CONTENTS

FOREWORD

Combustion. It happens when you strike a simple wooden match with enough friction to ignite the phosphorous coating on its red-and-white tip. The wood of the matchstick becomes the fuel to sustain it. The result? Heat and light.

As the small wooden stick burns, however, it is gradually consumed by the flame. Either that, or its supply of oxygen is cut off in an instant by merely blowing it out.

It's an easy analogy for what too often happens to all of us who start a new project, a new challenge, or a new career. We're excited. Highly motivated. We're "fired up." We're going to "bring the heat" or "blaze a trail." All of this inner energy fuels our white-hot ambition. Until it doesn't.

That's when our fuel runs out. Our proverbial oxygen supply is cut off. In a mere instant, exhaustion sets in. Disillusionment dismantles our vision. Weariness immobilizes our actions. And ultimately, burnout extinguishes our once-fiery excitement and motivation. No flame of passion. No fire in the belly. Not even a spark.

This is not metaphorical mumbo jumbo. The experience of feeling consumed by what once fueled your ambition is real. The World

Health Organization recently included the colloquial term "burn-out" in the International Classification of Diseases, and they call it an "occupational phenomenon."[1] In other words, if you're feeling burned out, it's not imaginary, and you're far from alone.

A recent survey of 15,000 workers across fifteen countries found that a quarter of all workers experienced burnout symptoms.[2] Burnout is at an all-time high across professions.[3]

We need help.

Enter my friend and colleague Dr. Jonathan Hoover. In *Stress Fracture*, Jonathan stands on a mountain of research that he's been scaling for years. Not only that, he integrates biblical wisdom to skillfully help all who are experiencing the ravages of burnout (or know a colleague or loved one who is). Jonathan speaks from the heart, and his message is sound and immeasurably practical.

This book will help you rekindle the passion you thought you'd lost. It will help you rediscover the heat and light you long for—personally and professionally. It will spark healing to mend your stress fractures.

Les Parrott, PhD
Seattle, Washington

1

Nietzsche or Goldilocks?

Years ago, I ended up on a midnight flight from Los Angeles to Dallas. Tired and slightly agitated by the cancelation of my direct flight home earlier in the day, I did my best to present a friendly demeanor to the passenger next to me, who apparently wanted to make small talk. He told me he was in the computer business and was flying to Dallas to see his wife and kids after being away for three weeks. He would be home for less than twenty-four hours before catching a red-eye flight to his next work appointment.

Trying to engage with what he was saying, I asked him why his schedule was so tight. He responded that his business had really taken off in the previous twelve months, bringing in tidal-wave profits and creating a crushing workload. Lately he'd been spending his days (and even some nights) putting out fires, calming the nerves of anxious board members, making key financial decisions, casting vision, hiring key personnel, traveling from worksite to worksite, gathering venture capital for new expansions, and baby-sitting the company's bottom line.

13

At this point, I was intrigued. "How do you manage to do all those things and still be physically and emotionally healthy?" I wondered if he actually was healthy. His response was classic:

"Well, you know what they say, What doesn't kill you makes you stronger." He forced a smile, but his weary eyes betrayed a lack of sleep.

"Are you sure that's true?"

His smile vanished, his gaze lowered—breaking our eye contact—and with a quiet, reserved tone, he answered, "No, but I hope so." As he said those words, he turned and faced the window, and I could see that our conversation had taken an unpleasant turn for my new computer-genius friend. He watched out the window as the runway lights of LAX flashed by and we lifted off.

It was time for a subject change. "What do you do?" he asked.

"I'm a pastor and a life coach," I said. "I specialize in helping distressed married couples and overextended leaders."

He seemed pleased at this and asked if I was willing to do some free life coaching. For the next hour, I listened and he talked.

While his business life couldn't be better, his personal life was a disappointment. His marriage was an example of this. It seemed that each time his business reached a new level of success, his marriage became more strained. He and his wife had previously had an exceptionally strong marriage, but things were different now. Over the past several months, they had begun to question whether they could stay together. Marriage was feeling hollow and pointless to him, and he felt like a constant disappointment to his wife. She often complained that she was tired of competing for his attention. She felt that the business had replaced her and she was getting his time-and-attention leftovers.

Meanwhile, he felt unappreciated. Why didn't she care that he was so successful? Why did she seem unhappy when he was working so hard?

The family stress wasn't limited to his marriage. He'd recently felt his kids growing away from him, too. Despite his hectic work life, he tried to be a good dad. He showed up at games, recitals, and performances whenever possible, and he tried to take a genuine interest in his kids' lives. But, as far as he could tell, it wasn't enough. Especially in the previous four or five months, he'd felt like an outsider at the dinner table when he was home. The kids didn't seem to have the same kind of drive to connect with him, and his attempts to bridge the divide weren't working. He sadly admitted, "When I travel now, I miss my kids more than I used to, but it seems like they miss me less."

Physically, he was a mess. He admitted that he wasn't eating smart, sleeping well, or taking good care of himself. And all this personal neglect was breaking his lifelong health streak. For most of his life, he'd managed to stay away from the doctor's office. He wasn't often sick, and even when he was, he recovered quickly and easily. But now he frequently struggled with this ailment or that, spending a lot of time in doctors' offices. As of late, he was often convinced that he must be sick, given how bad he was feeling. But while he was often scolded by doctors about his less-than-healthy lifestyle, he wasn't diagnosed with anything in particular. "Go figure," he said with a chuckle. "I'm finally convinced I'm sick, and they keep telling me I'm fine."

I watched a single tear chase down one side of his face. Pointing to it, he said, "And that's another thing! I cry now. I've never been a crier. What's up with that?"

He explained that he was often all over the page emotionally. He felt he was needlessly sharp with staff. He was easily agitated and frustrated, and it had become enough of a pattern that it was now bleeding over into his social life. "When I was just snapping at employees, I figured I was just doing what bosses have to do sometimes. But when I started snapping at friends, I knew something was out of whack."

Then he talked about anxiety. Lately, it had become a big problem. As of late, he was prone to irrational fears that would grow into mountains of worst-case-scenario anxieties that he didn't know how to address. He didn't talk much about them with others, though, because he didn't feel it was appropriate for leaders to be anxious. I remembered thinking that he must feel a tremendous amount of internal pressure.

Then the conversation took a brief spiritual turn. Since I mentioned that I was a pastor, I guess he felt obligated to share that he hadn't been to church in a long time. After meekly explaining that no one could maintain his schedule and attend services regularly, he lowered his voice and his gaze. "Maybe I'm too busy for God. I hope that's not really true."

I was struck by a sense of irony. After all, the flight had barely started when he paraphrased Nietzsche's idea that "what doesn't kill you makes you stronger." Somehow, this poor guy had come to believe that the way to achieve success in life is always to push harder. He seemed to be telling himself, *Keep going, because as long as you have a pulse, you have the capacity to do more, and doing more will eventually make you better.* But the reality was dark: this fellow had been pushing harder for a long time, and he was not better for it. He was worse.

We Know Better

If Nietzsche was right (or Kelly Clarkson, if you prefer), and what doesn't kill you always does make you stronger, then the higher your stress level the better. Right? If the logic holds true, then the more stress you endure, the better the payoff should be. Of course, the "what doesn't kill you" part seems a bit ominous. Even in this flawed logic, there seems to be a recognition that, at some point, the stress will kill you. And it surely will. But, for some reason, we seem to have bought into the idea that any stress that isn't fatal is beneficial in the long run. If we were to graph this absurd idea, we would have to put stress and reward on the same line—that's why I call the "what doesn't kill you makes you stronger" idea a linear view of stress. As you can see in the graph below, the more

Figure 1.1

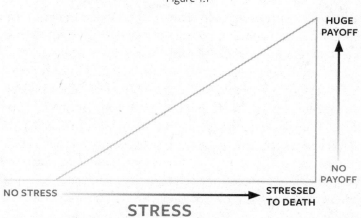

stress you manage to endure, the bigger the eventual payoff. That is, of course, until you make the unfortunate mistake of stressing yourself to death, at which point you get no benefit. If you take Nietzsche's idea to its logical end, a person gets the best results when they endure a near-fatal dose of stress. And we know better than that.

Frankly, I don't think any of us really believe that what doesn't kill you always makes you stronger. I think it's just a reassuring thing we tell ourselves when we know our stress load is getting out of hand. When the strain of our workload becomes nearly unbearable, it's a pleasant and calming thing to tell ourselves that we'll be better off in the end if we can just make it through. It's a way of resolving the cognitive dissonance we feel when we become aware of how much our stress load is really costing us but are unprepared to do anything about it. But we're not being honest with ourselves. After all, in nearly every other area of our lives, we'd laugh at the idea that there's no such thing as too much.

Most of us would actually argue that *too much of a good thing is a bad thing*, yet we seem to forget this when talking about stress. You may like a firm bed, but you're not about to start sleeping on a concrete slab. You might like the jolt you get from a caffeinated drink in the morning, but you're not likely to ingest pure caffeine (that can be fatal). You may like to have your extended family visit your home, but you're unlikely to ask them to live with you forever.

The truth is, when it comes to air conditioning in your home, wheatgrass in your protein shake, the volume level of your television set, and thousands of other things that influence your daily life, you probably tend to agree more with Goldilocks than Nietzsche. There is such a thing as too little, too much, and just right.

Pharmaceutical companies, who are legally required to respect the too-much-of-a-good-thing principle, try to find out two things when testing a new drug. First, they want to know how much of the drug needs to be administered for it to be even slightly *effective*. Obviously, if you have a headache and take only a small fraction of the recommended dosage, you're unlikely to feel better. The drug company needs to know how much of the drug is needed for it to work at all. Once they find that number, they know at what dosage the drug is *beneficial*.

Then they keep moving the dosage up in tests until they find out how much of the drug it takes to start producing unpleasant side effects or for it to simply quit working. At that point, even though the drug had previously been *beneficial*, a line has been crossed, and now it is *detrimental*.

Stress works the same way. There is a level at which stress is beneficial (sometimes stress in these amounts is called *eustress* or, literally, good stress), but if you overdose on stress, it becomes detrimental (*distress* or, literally, bad stress).

Here's another way of thinking about good stress and bad stress: if we were to graph the truth about that stress-to-payoff relationship I was talking about earlier, *we wouldn't get a straight line. We'd get a bell curve.*[1]

On the left side of the curve, where a person experiences no stress, they experience the physical and emotional aftermath of futility. With no good stress they can become lethargic, depressed,

Figure 1.2

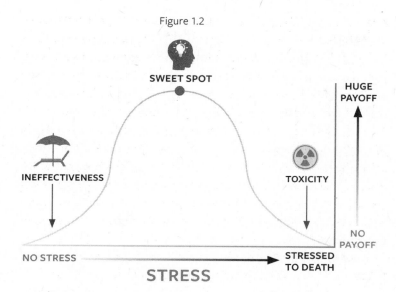

SWEET SPOT

HUGE
PAYOFF

INEFFECTIVENESS

TOXICITY

NO
PAYOFF

NO STRESS

STRESSED
TO DEATH

STRESS

and even sick. But as we experience a reasonable amount of good stress, and as we lean into the challenge, our performance gets better. *And, for most of us, especially if we love what we do, the feeling of leaning into the stress and getting incrementally better is addictive.* The problem is that it's tempting to believe that it will always work that way.

But once you reach the top of the stress curve in the chart above, a very dangerous, silent change takes place. Now, if you push harder, you will get worse results. The thing that has always boosted your performance (taking on more stress) will now kill your performance. Here's why: when you experience stress, your body gears up to handle the challenge. And, specifically, your nervous, immune, endocrine, cardiovascular, and musculoskeletal systems (as well as others) prescribe chemicals, hormones, and physical changes to meet the incoming demands.[2] But, as is the case with any prescription, there is a danger if the dosage gets out of hand.

Earlier I talked about how drug companies work to find the right dosage of drugs in order to be beneficial. We can use that same example to understand how that bell curve really works. Suppose you approach your doctor about some muscle pain you've been having, and your doctor prescribes twenty milligrams of a drug that should relax your muscles and help your body recover. If you decide not to follow the doctor's instructions, and instead only take one milligram of the drug, chances are you won't experience much relief. In the graphic above, the act of taking such a small amount of the medicine would put you on the ineffective side of the curve.

If, on the other hand, you decided to take four hundred milligrams of the drug, you might die. In the graph above, that would correspond with the toxicity idea. It's important to remember that a good thing, such as our body's natural response to stress, can become highly toxic if we get too much of it.

Put simply, if the dose of stress in our lives is too high, we get poorer results.

Perhaps I'm belaboring the point, but here's one more example of this fundamental concept: think about what happens when you work out at the gym. A healthy workout routine puts your body under a strategic level of stress. You expect to gain a benefit when you lift a certain amount of weight or complete a certain number of repetitions of a specific exercise. You know that if you follow your strategic regimen and you give your body adequate recovery time between workouts, you will reap health benefits and you'll get stronger.

But, on the other hand, if you overdo it and push beyond your own reasonable limits, you go from strategic, good, healthy stress to bad, unhealthy, damaging stress. Lifting too much weight, for instance, or repeating lifting workouts too quickly without adequate rest in between actually stunts muscle growth rather than building it.

Professional athletes can be among the worst offenders of pushing their bodies past the good stress point and into the toxic, bad stress point. The unrelenting desire to win causes them to push incredibly hard during training—so hard that they reach past what they feel able to do. They call this, not surprisingly, *overreaching*.[3] In the past couple of decades, some have determined that overreaching can be good for an athlete if it is coupled with great nutrition, substantial rest, and reasonable limits. This is called *functional overreaching.*

Functional overreaching is the sweet spot at the top of the bell curve. It's at this level that a person is pushing themselves just a bit beyond the comfortable reach of their natural capabilities. But athletes who are functionally overreaching make sure to *rest like they stress*, giving their body an opportunity to recover from the strain. Both elements are crucial to finding your own sweet spot on the stress curve. If you're in the sweet spot, *your stress load should stretch you a bit, but not crush you.* And *you must rest like you stress.* The heavier your stress load, the more careful you will have to be about giving your mind and body a chance to recover.

Unfortunately, a lot of athletes push past the sweet spot, not getting the recuperative nutrients and recovery time they need. When they make this mistake, it can stunt their ability so severely that some overstressed athletes have to take a break from the sport they love. When an athlete pushes too hard or ignores their physical need for recovery, this is called *nonfunctional overreaching*, and it is considered a very serious career threat. If a person continues in a pattern of nonfunctional overreaching, the day may come when he or she reaches a point called *overtraining*, in which their entire body pays the price for pushing too hard—often resulting in illness or depression. Some overtrained athletes find they are never able to return to their sport, at least not at a professional level.

And, because this condition has caused many exceptional talents to walk away from their athletic careers, there is now an official name for the phenomenon. It's called *overtraining syndrome.*[4] And it's a huge risk for athletes who are in the process of rising to the top.

When a rising Olympic swimming star is working out in the pool, it's tempting to try to survive just another thirty laps, even after their body has told them to stop an hour ago. It's tempting for the cyclist to push themselves to get in twenty more miles when their legs are stiffening up and their heart rate is becoming erratic. And, if they were to have any thoughts that doing so might not be wise, they may tell themselves that what doesn't kill them will make them stronger.

The sadder-but-wiser overtrained athlete will tell you the truth: *what doesn't kill you may almost kill you.* And it can certainly make you sick and take away your ability to do what you love.

It's easy to believe that the biggest trophies are won by the people who push themselves beyond their own limits—people who demand nearly superhuman performances from themselves. But the truth is, *better results don't happen past the sweet spot.*

If the bell-curve model of stress is correct (and it is), then we can assume that the best possible outcomes for a top performer (athletic or otherwise) happen at the top of the curve—they happen at the optimum amount of stress. *When a person pushes past the sweet spot, they get worse results—it's as simple as that.* In essence, when a person pushes too hard, they pass the hump of the curve and end up in the toxicity zone. Unfortunately, a lot of people don't understand that the reason they're starting to underperform is that they're pushing too hard; instead, they assume they're not pushing hard enough. So they demand more of themselves, hoping to fix the problem, and, sadly, they only make it worse.

Depending on how stressed you are, *you may have to quit pushing so hard to get better results.* It sounds backward, but it's true.

I shared this idea with my late-night travel companion as we winged our way toward Dallas, and he mulled it over. "But, if I really am on the toxic side of the curve, why is my business doing so well?" he asked. It was a reasonable question.

Actually, it's not uncommon for at least one part of your life to be going quite well even if you're far too stressed. Sadly, success in that one area can give you false reassurance, causing you to believe that everything is really okay. If you want to understand what kind of impact stress is having on your life, you must zoom out and look at your *gross personal product*.

Your Gross Personal Product

As I talked with my new friend on the plane, I pushed aside my airline peanuts and scribbled six letters on my napkin—P E R S O N. "You're not just a businessman," I reminded him, "you're a person. So there's more than just one area of your life where results matter."

Then I finished writing the words related to each of the letters.

Physical

Emotional

Relational

Spiritual

Occupational

Navigational

Next, I had him score each item. I asked him, "How happy are you with how you feel physically, on a scale of 1 to 10?"

"About a 3, I guess," he responded. We went on to score the other items. On a scale of 1 to 10, he rated his emotional wellness at 2. When I asked him how he was doing relationally, including work, family, and friend relationships, he scored it a 3. Spiritually, he scored himself a 2. Occupationally, he said he was doing very well—a 9. And navigationally (which represents how much a person likes the direction they're headed in life and feels the power to positively impact their future), he rated himself a 2.

Here's what his graph looked like.

See the problem? Sure, his work life might score a 9, but if you average his scores on all six areas of his life, you get a number I call his gross personal product, and that score is a 3. This is not

Figure 1.3

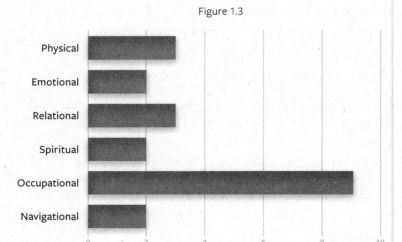

the graph of a healthy life. This graph says, *At work, I'm killing it. Away from work, I'm getting killed.* This graph says, *I'm in limp mode.*

Limp Mode

Under the hood of my car is a very smart computer. It tells the spark plugs when to fire, it decides how much fuel to send to the injectors, and it monitors how much air is getting sucked in through the intake manifold. Unlike older cars, a microcomputer decides how to best utilize the elements of combustion—air, fuel, and spark—to make my car-driving experience efficient, reliable, and enjoyable. As long as the system works properly, it makes decisions based on what is efficient.

However, if sensors quit working or the computer malfunctions, the car will go into what is often called *limp mode.* In this mode, the car knows that something is really wrong. At that point the goal of the car changes. Instead of efficiency, the goal now is simply to keep the engine running until the car can get to the nearest automotive shop. In limp mode, the algorithm is not designed to promote *smart choices*, it's designed to promote *survival.*

That's what's happening in the PERSON chart earlier. This guy is unquestionably in limp mode. When he crossed over into the toxic zone, a part of him became aware that if he tried to be at a 9 in all the areas of his life, he'd be stalled out on the side of the road. So he's long since given up being efficient. Now he's just doing whatever it takes to survive. He maintains that high score at work, but he's taking a major hit everywhere else.

Here's the problem with limp mode: as long as we can keep limping, it's tempting to believe everything's okay. Many folks have ruined their engines because they didn't realize how urgently their car needed attention when it was in limp mode. They saw the check engine light. They felt the sluggishness when they stepped on the gas. But they were still rolling down the road. And, as long as they were rolling, they weren't concerned. But *survival mode is never a long-term strategy.* My new friend on that flight needed to know that the longer he stayed in limp mode, the more likely it would be that his 9 at work would start dropping. Eventually, the whole graph would bottom out if he didn't do something about it.

What Are the Options?

So far, I've only really shared theoretical information with you, and there's more theory to come, but there's also a practical question we should start addressing right now. What are the options for my new computer-genius friend, whom I met on this late-night flight? He's obviously burned out, way past the sweet spot of peak performance, and stuck in limp mode, so what should he do?

And what should you do if you're burned out?

To answer that question, let's think back to the example of working out at the gym. Suppose one day you determine you've been pushing yourself far too hard, and it's causing counterproductive results. Perhaps you've been lifting weights, but instead of getting positive results, you're noticing that your body is overfatigued and strained. If that's the case, you have three options. First, you could decide to lift less weight. Second, you could choose to lift the weight in a different way. Or, finally, you could make healthy choices outside the gym that could help you be better prepared to lift at the gym.

These three options are available for an overstressed person like the gentlemen I talked to on the plane. First, he could decide to reduce his stress level. This, among the three strategies, is usually the toughest sell. Most of us don't think many items on our agenda could possibly be eliminated—even though that's simply not true.

Most of us are very capable of trimming down our stress loads without the world cataclysmically coming to an end. Don't worry, though, I'll never try to convince you to settle for poor results, and I won't suggest you learn to be happy with mediocrity. My promise is this: any time we talk about *reducing the weight* you're lifting, it'll be for the purpose of *increasing your gross personal product*, not reducing it.

Sometimes, of course, it's not an option to reduce the weight you're lifting. When that's the case, it pays to step back and consider *how* you lift. Sometimes the most practical, positive step you can take is to approach the weight of stress differently. Just as I might strain my muscles lifting weights at the gym if the seat is not adjusted properly on the machine, or if I don't use the right group of muscles to carry the weight, it is possible for the burden of daily stress to be made worse because of the way we approach it. The adjustments we may need to make can seem small, but in the end, they can pay off big time.

Finally, just as I might have more success at the gym if I chose not to down a dozen Krispy Kreme donuts and a two-liter of soda right before my workout, many of us could take a stronger position against stress if we made just a few healthy life choices to combat its effects. This final, practical step is the universally applicable one. We can't always reduce the weight we lift, and sometimes there are no adjustments to be made. But we can always step up our game in terms of healthy life choices.

The rest of this book will focus on using these three approaches to get your life back. In the chapters ahead, we'll talk about how you can win the battle against burnout and get back into the sweet spot—physically, emotionally, relationally, spiritually, occupationally, and navigationally.

CHAPTER 1

Small Group Discussion Questions

1. What's your personal take on the idea that "what doesn't kill you makes you stronger"?
2. Have you ever pushed yourself beyond the sweet spot of stress? What was that like for you?
3. Earlier we talked about limp mode. Limp mode happens in life when we don't have enough energy to be efficient, so our energy goes toward survival. Have you ever had a time when you were in limp mode? How did that impact your work and personal life? How did you get out of limp mode?
4. We also talked about the difference between good stress and bad stress. What are some examples of good stress and bad stress in your life?
5. How does a Christian best live out these two realities: 1) we are finite and have limited energy, and 2) we serve an infinite God?

Are You Burned Out?

1. I dread going to work.

Strongly Agree	Agree	Neutral	Disagree	Strongly Disagree
5	4	3	2	1

2. People have really started to make me tired.

Strongly Agree	Agree	Neutral	Disagree	Strongly Disagree
5	4	3	2	1

3. I've started feeling down about myself at work, or down about my workplace.

Strongly Agree	Agree	Neutral	Disagree	Strongly Disagree
5	4	3	2	1

4. I've been more forgetful lately.

Strongly Agree	Agree	Neutral	Disagree	Strongly Disagree
5	4	3	2	1

5. I've noticed that I am more impulsive than I used to be.

Strongly Agree	Agree	Neutral	Disagree	Strongly Disagree
5	4	3	2	1

6. Lately I check out mentally or daydream at work more than I used to.

Strongly Agree	Agree	Neutral	Disagree	Strongly Disagree
5	4	3	2	1

7. It's easier for me to be frustrated with people than it used to be.

Strongly Agree	Agree	Neutral	Disagree	Strongly Disagree
5	4	3	2	1

8. I've been more anxious or worrisome lately, especially at or about work.

Strongly Agree	Agree	Neutral	Disagree	Strongly Disagree
5	4	3	2	1

9. At work, I look at other people I work with and think, *They have no idea how stressed I am.*

Strongly Agree	Agree	Neutral	Disagree	Strongly Disagree
5	4	3	2	1

10. It's almost impossible for me to de-stress at home.

Strongly Agree	Agree	Neutral	Disagree	Strongly Disagree
5	4	3	2	1

11. I think I'm more emotionally reactive than I used to be.

Strongly Agree	Agree	Neutral	Disagree	Strongly Disagree
5	4	3	2	1

12. If I went on a restful vacation for a week, I'd be truly depressed at the thought of going back to work at the end of the vacation.

Strongly Agree	Agree	Neutral	Disagree	Strongly Disagree
5	4	3	2	1

13. When I think of things that might help me de-stress (for instance, delegating tasks or taking time off), there are reasons why none of them can happen.

Strongly Agree	Agree	Neutral	Disagree	Strongly Disagree
5	4	3	2	1

14. I think my stress is causing disconnection in relationships that are important to me.

Strongly Agree	Agree	Neutral	Disagree	Strongly Disagree
5	4	3	2	1

15. I feel like I just don't have the energy to keep going.

Strongly Agree	Agree	Neutral	Disagree	Strongly Disagree
5	4	3	2	1

HOW TO SCORE THIS SURVEY:

Add up all the numbers you circled. Then check your score with the following table.

15–40	41–50	51–65	66–75
No/Low Burnout	Moderate Burnout	High Burnout	Extreme Burnout

*This table is not scientifically validated; it is for use only as a rule of thumb.

Super Rats

In chapter 1, I talked about a conversation I had on a flight with a burned-out, overextended businessman. That story is from quite some time ago. Since then, I received my PhD in organizational psychology, and—in addition to my ministry and university faculty responsibilities—I have begun a career as a burnout researcher. Looking back on that conversation, I feel certain that the main issue this fellow was dealing with was a major case of burnout. The term *burnout* is, of course, a great word picture for his condition. The images of a spent light bulb or a burned match spring to mind. This poor guy was very much like the bulb that won't light because its energy is used up. But, after reading this chapter, I think you'll have an even deeper understanding of why I think the fellow on the plane was burned out. Especially when you understand the theory of super rats.

Okay, so that's my term . . . *super rats*. It comes from an experiment conducted by Hans Selye, who is revered as the father of modern stress science.[1] He is even largely responsible for coining the term *stress* in the way you and I use it today. When he wrote his original academic work, there wasn't really a term that fit the bill, so he used the term *noxious agents*.[2] I'm glad he came up with something a bit catchier. Selye is famous for studying stress in animals like rats to learn ways in which human beings might also respond to stress. He did tons of these experiments, and six decades later his work is still foundational for anyone wanting to understand the science of stress and burnout.

One of Selye's lesser-known experiments has always fascinated me, especially as I've become more focused on studying burnout: Selye sometimes used temperature to stress out the rats, and at one point he took some of the rats in his lab and placed them into a near-freezing refrigerator.[3] At first the rats struggled to adjust to the extreme cold, but after a while, they began to thrive in it. Their little bodies developed ways to combat the cold, like storing larger amounts of fat beneath their skin and growing thicker coats. They became what I like to call *super rats*. Even though they initially struggled with the cold, they eventually adapted to handle it.

In this process of adaptation, the rats' bodies adjusted to the stressful demands of the environment, and they were able to function in a less-than-ideal situation. Then, Selye got really creative. He took some of the super rats and put them in an even colder environment. Selye already knew that if he took regular rats and put them in this super-cold environment they died. But, interestingly, the super rats lived. At least, they lived for a while. Their adaptation helped them survive longer in an environment that would be fatal to their peers. But, after several weeks, the super rats would reach a point at which the adaptation couldn't keep up. And they died. Interestingly, even if one of the super rats was moved out of the super-cold refrigeration at this point of burnout and returned to the less-cold refrigeration, they still died.

Okay, so how does this apply to you? Like the super rats, you have the ability to adapt to stressful environments. At first you may really struggle with a very stressful situation, but often you will find yourself adjusting to it in time. And eventually you may appear to be extremely successful at handling the stress that comes your way. You're adapting. But what the super rats story teaches us is that adaptation energy is a limited resource. You only have so much ability to adapt. After a certain point, there is no more adjusting room, and you experience the full weight of the stress. That's usually when collapse happens. That's when burnout happens.

And Dr. Selye learned with his super rats that it's not enough in a moment of burnout to just back off the stress a little bit. You will have to completely back away from the stress long enough to figure out how you will approach what was apparently *too much for too long*. It's only then that you will have the ability to restart the process of adapting well to the stress of life.

If you want to see Dr. Selye's theories at work in your own life, you can probably do it just by looking back over the course of some stressful role in your life. Whether that role was as a boss, a parent, a caregiver, or something else, you probably initially felt like you wouldn't be able to handle it. Dr. Selye called that stage of stress *alarm*.[4] It is the stage of stress that tells us that we are faced with something bigger than we can comfortably handle.

First-year college students often go through a phase of alarm in the first days of being away from home. The separation from parents and the new life of higher-level classes, schedules, and unfamiliar buildings often converge to create anxiety. Over the years, many parents have had to talk their young student out of hopping on a plane and coming right back home, where life may not have been so overwhelmingly stressful. The reason parents encourage their kids to stay rather than come home is because they know that after a few days, the stress will be replaced by a new normal. The student will learn where the buildings are located. They will get comfortably settled in classes, and they will learn to thrive away from home. That's the stage that Dr. Selye called *adaptation*. As we discussed earlier, that's the stage that separates rats from super rats.

It's Dr. Selye's third stage of stress that I'm particularly inter-ested in, as are other burnout researchers. It's the stage called *exhaustion*. Not everybody gets stressed out enough to make it to that stage. For instance, the college students I mentioned in the last paragraph hopefully will not hit this third level of stress. Hope-fully, as they adapt they will not push themselves so hard that they run out of energy to adapt. But some people do just that. They begin to take the ability to adapt for granted. And when they do, they spend all the adaptation energy they have and run completely out of the internal resources they need to battle stress.

When I think of taking the ability to adapt for granted, I think of a friend I had in college who had well-to-do parents. They loaded a monthly sum of money on a check card for him to use for expenses while he was away at college. He never asked them how much they loaded on the card, and I don't think he ever bothered to monitor how much was being deposited. When he needed money, it always seemed to be there, and so he spent it. Over time he became more aggressive with his spending, and I remember the day that he tried to make a purchase and was declined because he had spent more than was deposited. He was shocked. It was as though he had imagined that there would never be a time when he would need more money than he had. What a perfect metaphor for this idea of adaptation energy!

Every day we wake up with new energy to take on challenges and difficulties, but it's not unlimited energy. Some of us act like it is, though. Some of us expend more adaptation energy every day, continually pushing ourselves harder, expecting that we will be able to adapt to anything that comes our way. That's not true. Eventually you will go to the well, and it will be dry. The check will bounce, so to speak, and you will find that you have bargained for more than you can reasonably handle. And that moment of exhaustion comes with some nasty features. Like the super rats, you will find that you are not able to just shake off exhaustion. You won't be able to cancel a couple of meetings or take an overnight trip and snap out of it. Exhaustion is a serious thing. It requires a major change in the way that we view the resource of adaptation energy. We have to start thinking of it like the allowance I mentioned earlier. Yes, the energy to adapt is a renewable resource. It's just not an infinite resource.

What Does Burnout Look Like?

Most of what we know about burnout came to us by way of one of the most well-known researchers in stress psychology: Dr. Christina Maslach. What I'm about to share with you is not original to me (the following headings of *emotional exhaustion, depersonalization,* and *reduced feelings of accomplishment* are her terms), so if you want to understand burnout, here's a short primer.

Burnout happens because of unregulated stress over a period of time (too much for too long). And usually that stress happens in the context of working with people. That's important because *burnout is just as much a relational problem as it is a personal one.* It impacts how you deal with others. In fact, that's what caused burnout science to get its start. Dr. Maslach was interested in the fact that some workers in people-facing occupations (lawyers, physicians, welfare workers, etc.) became exhausted and lost their ability to give of themselves to their clients over time, and eventually they grew withdrawn from and discouraged about their work. While observing this dynamic, she noticed that burnout was a bidirectional problem, harming both the exhausted individual, who had nothing left to give, and the people they needed to serve.[5] So, for example, the burned-out lawyer pays a price because he feels too exhausted to pick up the phone and call his client. And the client pays a price because her lawyer is mentally absent without leave. This is why I'm passionate about studying burnout myself: when a person is burned out, everyone loses. And we now know that burnout is contagious,[6] so I would make the case that it's not just about the consumer and the provider, it's also about the community. We must get a grip on burnout or our world suffers. Here's what it looks like.

Emotional Exhaustion

Dr. Maslach's work indicates that the first and most important part of burnout is a sort of exhaustion of our emotional energy.[7] Remember that we all have a sort of adaptation energy that is a finite resource. The most relevant energy in this discussion is the emotional energy to adapt. The stress of life is, perhaps more than anything else, an *emotional* battle that we fight daily. When our stress load is reasonable, we have enough adaptation energy to sort through the emotional soup that comes along with the stress. We know from neuropsychology that for those who have particularly strong executive-functioning brain capacity, the emotional battle of stress may even be somewhat below one's awareness.[8] In other words, you may not even know that you're fighting major emotional battles while you still have energy to fight them. Once you run out of energy, you'll feel them—in a big way.

Sometimes I talk to people who tell me that they struggle with depression or anxiety. Usually by that they mean that they have been diagnosed with a major depressive disorder or one of the several anxiety disorders in the Diagnostic and Statistics Manual of the American Psychiatry Association (the Bible of mental disorders). But the truth is, while not all of us deal with these challenges at a clinical level, we *all* struggle to some extent with anxiety and depression. There is a battle going on in our brains on a daily basis between anxiety and confidence and between depression and pleasant motivation. Emotional energy allows us to fight that daily battle and, for the most part, win.

And like the super rats I talked about earlier, some of us have developed much more emotional energy than what we started with. Different life circumstances we've faced originally alarmed us, but we developed the emotional energy to carry on. And now, to others, we might look almost superhuman. They might look at the challenges we are able to survive on a daily basis and surmise, perhaps correctly, that others wouldn't be able to bear up under that type of stress. For instance, you might be caring for an elderly parent. And people around you might be amazed at the mental fortitude you show every day to take care of your loved one with patience, love, and support. And if you were to step back for a moment, you'd probably be amazed, too. There certainly would have been a time in your life when you wouldn't have been capable of doing this. But you've developed the needed strength to make this happen. Just be careful. Adaptation energy is a finite resource. And there is such a thing as *too much*.

What do we mean by *emotional exhaustion*? First, it's important to distinguish the idea of exhaustion from being tired. I might come home from a long day at work and tell my wife, "I'm exhausted." But what I really mean is, "I'm tired." Exhaustion, at least in this case, means to be totally spent. It means to be used up. To be emotionally exhausted is the emotional equivalent of being stuck on the side of the road because you have run completely out of gas. So, as you can imagine, when a person completely runs out of emotional energy, they struggle to do things like experience the feelings they would expect to feel under normal circumstances.[9] They struggle to be aware of the feelings they do experience, and most importantly, they struggle to regulate the emotions that surface.[10]

Earlier, I used the term *battle* to describe emotion regulation. Another word we could use is *balance*. Our brain, because of the amazing way God designed it, is able to help us strike a balance between feeling emotions and being absorbed by them. To feel sadness in appropriate ways at appropriate times is a wonderful thing. To be absorbed by sadness can be a very destructive thing. Similarly, if I could forfeit my ability to ever be angry, I wouldn't do it. How else would I know how and when to stand against injustice? On the other hand, I certainly would not want anger to take control of my life. Emotional exhaustion means losing that balance.

Emotions suddenly become unpredictable, unhelpful, and very difficult to regulate.

A person dealing with emotional exhaustion may toggle from feeling numb to feeling extreme emotion. They may show signs of depression, unable to enjoy things they once loved. They may start to be far more mercurial, losing their temper over small things in one moment and sometimes showing almost childlike anxiety the next. In moments where they would have once showed compassion, reaching out to another person to show care and sympathy, they may sit statue-like, staring off into the distance. Or they may become highly critical of themselves or others, causing new relationship problems that didn't exist before they became exhausted. Regardless, a few things are certain: emotional exhaustion makes individuals less predictable in their emotional responses to life, it makes them less able to handle the curveballs life throws their way, and it makes them less relationally healthy. And this can lead to depersonalization.

Depersonalization

At the point where we have no more emotional energy to give, we start to become less of the person we used to be.[11] We begin to give less of ourselves, to be less present, and to withdraw from the stress, even if that withdrawal has some pretty hefty consequences. For instance, a stay-at-home parent who is burned out and experiencing this stage of depersonalization may still carry on with the tasks associated with caring for their kids and the household, but they may do it mindlessly, and the warm, caring self they used to be may be replaced with an almost robotic self. There is certainly a business-as-usual season of depersonalization when the tasks still get done, but the person is no longer fully present. Eventually, the tasks will start to fall through the cracks as well. The paperwork that used to be done perfectly will be riddled with mistakes, the perfect attendance record will be ruined by no-call, no-show mornings, or some other stressful task will go undone or sloppily done. Then, sadly, the consequences of depersonalization become obvious to the burned-out person. And at that point they will experience the next stage of burnout—reduced feelings of accomplishment.

Reduced Feelings of Accomplishment

When you've spent your life being good at things, you're not used to facing personal failure. And when you do face failure, you adjust and get better. Remember the concept of adaptation we discussed earlier? You've probably spent much of your life adapting to failure, quickly adjusting, and getting better when something doesn't work. But imagine being faced with your own failure and realizing that you don't have the ability to adapt and change. As we discussed earlier, when you're burned out, you're out of energy to adapt when things go wrong. So for a burned-out person, it's terribly painful to stare at the consequences of tasks gone wrong—tasks you would once have done well—and know that you don't have the energy to fix the problem.[12]

In those moments, the addictive feelings of success that used to make you feel so good are replaced with the debilitating feelings that come with shame. In that moment, it is normal for a burned-out person to feel useless, to feel there is no hope for the future, and to become depressed and even sometimes suicidal.[13] What makes this stage of burnout particularly difficult is that often feelings of reduced accomplishment are not irrational. Sometimes we're not accomplishing much when we're burning out. And that makes sense. Remember the normal curve we talked about in chapter 1? We talked about how, once past the sweet spot, you get worse results and not better ones. The depersonalization and reduced feelings of accomplishment that happen when you're burned out are really the result of pushing past the sweet spot and having to face the consequences. When that happens, you're likely to feel like a failure—even when there is plenty of evidence to suggest you've been successful before.

Putting It Together

Now, as a researcher in the field of burnout psychology, I think back on the fellow in the airplane I talked about in chapter 1, and it's not hard to see all three of these stages of burnout present—the emotional exhaustion, the depersonalization, and the reduced feelings of personal accomplishment. No wonder this fellow, successful though he was at work, knew he needed to talk to someone. He knew he needed help. Whether he realized he was burned out or not, he knew that the way he had been living life was not working and he needed to make a change. Perhaps as you're reading, you're seeing how burnout is something you or someone you love is struggling with. Maybe you are starting to realize that you can't keep pushing yourself as hard as you have been. Perhaps you're ready to make a change. If so, I hope this book inspires you to fight the battle against burnout and find a new normal. But before we move on, let's take a moment to consider a case of burnout from the Bible. If you are not a believer and want to skip ahead, please feel free to do so. But even if you are not a Christian, you may find the next section helpful.

Burnout in the Bible?

It may help you to know that one of the most godly characters of the Old Testament struggled with such a bad case of burnout that he was, at least in a manner of speaking, suicidal. In the book of 1 Kings, the prophet Elijah was God's messenger to his people, Israel. At the time, Israel had a train wreck of a king named Ahab. The Bible tells us that Ahab was the worst king Israel ever had (see 1 Kings 16), and his wife, Jezebel, was worse than he was. There's a reason few of us name our sons Ahab or our daughters Jezebel. Neither were role models. They were both self-absorbed, narcissistic, and abusive. And Elijah, being God's messenger, wasn't on their good list.

To understand the story, it's important to know that Elijah's life was stressful from the moment he became a prophet. He was always in danger of Ahab and Jezebel's violent aggression, and he often had to trust the Lord for basic living needs like food, water, and shelter. The guy had to handle stress all the time. But in chapter 18 of 1 Kings, Elijah is facing a particularly stressful moment. The people of Israel are willing to listen to what Elijah has to say about God, but they also like to listen to Jezebel's prophets, who served the fake god Baal, the god of prosperity and sex. Like Christians today, it was easy for God's people to waffle between following the true God and serving sex or money. Elijah needed to put a stop to that.

So he decided that there needed to be some way he could show the people of Israel that God was real and Baal was fake. He challenged the 450 prophets of Baal to a contest on Mount Carmel, where two altars were constructed. A bull was placed on each altar, and the deal Elijah cut was that both he and the prophets of Baal would pray to have fire sent down from heaven on their respective sacrifices. Whoever sent down the fire would obviously be God, and the matter would be settled. It's a fascinating story with tons of exciting details, so I challenge you to read it sometime. It turned out this way, though—after a day of the prophets of Baal calling fire down from heaven, nothing happened. Not even a spark. Afterward, when Elijah prayed, fire came down from heaven and consumed the sacrifice and the altar, leaving a scorched mark where the altar used to be. That was a big win for Elijah. Afterward, Elijah killed the prophets of Baal and announced that God would end the drought that had been creating a famine. Again, it was a pretty big day for Elijah.

You'd think the stress of that day was over. You'd think that if Elijah was going to have a breakdown, or if he was going to become burned out, it would have happened during the middle of that intense day. But it didn't. Later, when word made it to Jezebel that Elijah had killed her prophets, she fired off a message to him to let him know that she planned to kill him for revenge. Keep in mind, Elijah had always been dealing with threats from Ahab and Jezebel. That was nothing new. And you'd think that, bolstered by his success on Mount Carmel, he'd be more able than ever to laugh off Jezebel's threat. From a Christian perspective, we would expect that Elijah would trust God to protect him and keep him safe. We don't expect Elijah to suddenly have a breakdown at this moment. *But he does.* Isn't it interesting that the breakdown moment often comes *after* the time of extreme stress, rather than during it?

But it makes sense if you remember the super rats. Remember that they initially live just fine in the coldest of environments in the experiment. But there will be a moment when you'll write an adaptation energy check that will bounce. No one will be there to announce ahead of time that you've gone too far for too long. It won't always make sense. Sometimes it will happen after the big stressor is over, without any particular last straw. Sometimes the last straw will be something trivial and inconsequential. In the end, when you're out of energy to adapt, you're out. And Elijah was out.

If you want to see the biblical picture of burnout, just read 1 Kings chapter 19. Elijah, burned out and spent, travels far outside the territory God has called him to. He withdraws from his work. We discussed this sort of withdrawal earlier when we talked about depersonalization. He heads toward a wilderness, which is a very apt picture for what depersonalization is like—it is like a withdrawal to a wilderness of self-preservation. He withdraws from people completely; in the last town he passes through on the way to the wilderness, he leaves his servant behind. Emotionally exhausted and completely withdrawn from his calling, he finds a spot in the wilderness to die and asks God to kill him. He tells God, "I have had enough" (1 Kings 19:4). That is the emotional exhaustion talking. Then he tells God that he has failed—in his words, he says, "I am no better than my ancestors" (v. 4), which is the reduced feelings of personal accomplishment coming through.

And he reiterates that he wishes to die, which is the ultimate de-personalization—a withdrawal from life.

Elijah falls asleep, which is probably an indicator of how much he had neglected his need for rest. An angel wakes him up, has prepared food for him, and instructs him to eat. This is probably an indication that Elijah had been neglecting his diet as well. After eating, Elijah goes back to sleep, and when he wakes up, the angel makes him eat again! Afterward, God instructs Elijah to meet him on a specific mountain. On the mountain, Elijah once again tells God what a failure he is. God responds with some very powerful demonstrations of his power.

God first sent a windstorm that sheared rocks loose from the mountain. Then he sent an earthquake (a scary thing to experience if you're standing on a mountain). Finally, God sent a fire. Scripture is clear that God himself was not in the windstorm, though, nor was he in the earthquake or the fire. The wording suggests that Elijah expected God to be in one of those.

I remember being at Bible college and hearing all the complicated explanations my professors had for the symbolism of the windstorm, the earthquake, and the fire. Frankly, I don't think there's any deep symbolism. I think Elijah was a person who was used to getting what he prayed for. After all, he prayed for God to send down fire from heaven on a sacrifice, and it happened. So when he prayed for his own death, I have to think he expected death to soon follow. That's why I say I believe he was truly suicidal. This wasn't some sort of spiritual melodrama . . . this was a serious request for death.

I think when the windstorm hit, Elijah expected God to be in the windstorm, and he expected that he was going to die at that moment. When that didn't happen, I think Elijah must have expected to die in the earthquake or the fire. But God was not in either of those. I believe the message God was sending with those demonstrations of his power was this: *If I wanted to take you out, I have a lot of ways I could make that happen. You're here for a reason.*

Eventually God came to Elijah in the form of a "still small voice" (1 Kings 19:12 KJV). The voice asked the question God had asked him multiple times: "What are you doing here?" (1 Kings 19:13).

I've pondered that question a lot as I've studied burnout. What did God mean when he asked Elijah, "What are you doing here?" Here's what I've come to. I think that God wanted Elijah to know this was not the right place for him to be, and there was a better place within his reach. And perhaps that's what you need to hear as you finish out this chapter. God has bigger plans for you than sitting on the sidelines of burnout. You have a future, and you can be more successful than ever before. Sure, it probably means making changes, but there is a better place for you, metaphorically speaking.

When God gave Elijah instructions, they involved changes. First God told Elijah to "go back the same way you came." God instructed Elijah to realize he had taken some steps in the wrong direction, and to intentionally reverse those negative steps. For many people reading this book, you will have to "go back the same way you came" (1 Kings 19:15). I'd like to encourage you to rethink decisions you've made on the path that led you to this moment of burnout. You may have to use your own trail to walk back to the point at which your stress went from healthy to unhealthy.

The second instruction God gave Elijah was to anoint his successor, Elisha. Basically, God told Elijah that he would have to quit being a lone ranger and start leveraging relationships to help combat his stress load. Too many of us have the life motto that "if you want something done right, you've got to do it yourself." As a result, we're hesitant to delegate, to share, or to collaborate in handling stressful things, and we try to do it all ourselves. God didn't design us to live or work that way.

Finally, God wanted Elijah to embrace the truth. The truth was that Elijah wasn't a failure, and his life *was* making a difference. Elijah had convinced himself that he was the only God follower left and his life hadn't made a difference. God told Elijah that he had seven thousand people in Israel who were loyal to him. That meant two things. It meant that Elijah wasn't alone, and it meant that he had made a difference. Burnout has a way of predisposing us to believe untrue messages about our past and our future. It causes us to second-guess whether we were ever effective, and whether we ever can be again. But that's not the truth. You have made a difference. You can make a difference in the future. You *will* make a difference in the future. What are you doing here? It's time to get to a better place.

CHAPTER 2
Group Discussion Questions

1. Think of an example of stress in your life to which you've had to adapt. What did you learn in the process of adapting to that challenge?

2. Has there ever been a time in your life when you felt like your emotional energy was exhausted (and by exhausted, we mean totally spent)? What led up to that exhaustion? How did you deal with it?

3. What do you think about the idea of depersonalization? Have you ever seen someone basically withdraw from the best parts of themselves? What did you observe?

4. Do you think stress has ever caused you to feel like a failure or like you're letting people down? If so, how have you dealt with those discouraging thoughts?

5. We talked about how Elijah had a last-straw moment—the moment when Jezebel said she was out to get him. Have you ever had a last-straw moment? Share with the group.

Getting Your Life Back Physically

I can't prove it, but I'm convinced that burnout killed Edsel Ford. He was only forty-nine years old at the time of his death.[1] You might not be familiar with Edsel Ford, but you probably know a good bit about his dad, Henry. Henry Ford is the person we credit with building the first car that the American public could afford. His mechanical genius and manufacturing smarts gave us both the Model T (sometimes called the "Ford car") and the modern assembly line. Edsel was Henry Ford's only son, and he was thrust into the wild and stressful workplace of his father at a very young age. At twenty-five, Edsel became the president of Ford Motor Company.[2] Talk about stress . . . that means that by the time he was in his midforties, he had successfully shepherded one of the nation's largest manufacturing companies through the Great Depression. Those who watched him live out that responsibility say he did so with class, ingenuity, humility, and a collaborative spirit. And he did that all while dealing with the added stress of dealing with his father, Henry, who tended to habitually add difficulty to his already stressful life.[3]

Henry Ford still insisted on running the company from the shadows even though he was not president anymore.[4] And the old man's brilliance tended to be matched by his problematic eccentricity. During the years that Edsel was running Ford Motor Company, his dad created more problems for him than solutions. Here are just a few examples: Edsel knew that Ford needed to turn out new models of cars yearly like their competitors. The Model T, as wonderful as it was, was eventually outdated by the competition. But Henry loved the Model T and insisted that a new model wasn't needed.[5] Edsel was open to negotiating with organized labor, but Henry couldn't stand the idea.[6] The elder Ford was willing to fight it out with unions, even if it meant sponsoring violence. Edsel wanted to have a collaborative spirit in the workplace, so he looked for ways to find shared goals and mutually agreeable solutions in the senior team at Ford. But despite his hard work to create a collaborative and forward-thinking culture at Ford Motor Company, he was nearly always undermined in some way by Henry Ford's my-way-or-the-highway directives. And while, aside from his philanthropic and personal endeavors, Edsel wanted to focus on building and perfecting automobiles, Henry also wanted to focus on grandiose projects like politics, publishing, and social engineering.[7] Each of those projects ended up creating massive messes that Edsel was partially responsible to clean up afterward. Imagine what it must have been like to have the title of president of the Ford Motor Company but to have your hands tied behind the scenes by a stubborn, hypercritical, egotistical bully. The stress of that kind of situation will make you sick. And Edsel definitely did get sick. In my opinion, a daily, compounding load of overwhelming stress is what killed Edsel before he made it to his fiftieth birthday.

Chronic Stress

There's a term for that kind of stress Edsel was dealing with. We call it *chronic stress*. Unlike acute stressors that hit you quickly and dissipate quickly, chronic stressors don't resolve—they revolve. They hit you over and over again, time after time, weighing you down and tiring you out. A chronic stressor is that mentally exhausting thing that you carry around every day and can't avoid thinking about. It's one of the last things you think about before you go to bed, and it's a weight that settles on your shoulders as you get out of bed in the morning. Chronic stress is a burden you carry over time. And the longer you carry the burden, the heavier it seems to be.

Imagine this: suppose I ask you to hold your arm straight out in front of you. As you do that, I place a five-pound weight in your hand and tell you to keep your arm outstretched as you hold the weight. At first it will be well within your ability to do that. It's only five pounds. But not very many minutes after that, you will start to be distressed holding up that weight. You'll start sweating, your arm will begin to ache—it may start cramping—and after a bit, you will have to put the weight down.

That's the way chronic stress works. It's not just the weight that you carry that tends to create problems. It's the length of *time* you have to carry that weight. If, for instance, you have a health scare and have to wait for forty-eight hours to get your results from the doctor, the stress of that waiting will be significantly less than if you have to wait two weeks. The longer you carry a burden, the heavier it gets.

Burnout is the end result of chronic stress. When you carry too much for too long, something has to give. For a moment, think about that weight example I gave you earlier. Is it not true that there's a sort of mental shift that happens as you're holding that weight? At first you think, *I've got this. It's not too heavy.* Then you start to think, *Wow, this is getting really difficult.* And then there's that moment where your brain registers the impossibility of carrying that weight forever, and you think, *I'm going to have to figure something out here . . . I can't keep holding this.*

You'll have similar thoughts and feelings if you're dealing with chronic stress. In the beginning you may feel relatively sure you can keep going, holding the daily weight you carry on your shoulders. But then, as time goes on, you start realizing that it's taking a toll on you—especially on your health. But you soldier on. Then there is that moment when burnout really kicks in, and you realize you just can't go on as you have been in the past. It's not even that the weight has necessarily gotten heavier. It's just that carrying it for this long has put you in a place where you can't go on.

Back to the story of Edsel. If you search the internet for Edsel Ford's cause of death, you'll probably see either stomach ulcers or stomach cancer listed as the reason. He had both. And it's likely that his stomach ulcers eventually turned into stomach cancer, so that's the reason you might see either listed as a cause of death. Back in the mid-twentieth century, when Edsel died, stress was thought to be a cause of stomach ulcers, and so there was a lot of speculation that the stress of Edsel's life had killed him. In fact, some people (including Henry Ford's own wife, Clara) felt Henry was personally responsible for his son's death—at least to some extent.[8]

Of course, we know now that H. pylori bacteria cause many stomach ulcers. But don't discount the impact of stress yet. We also know that chronic stress makes you more vulnerable to getting stomach ulcers, that it makes ulcers slower to heal, and that it makes people more susceptible to certain forms of cancer.[9] So, while I can't prove it, I think it probably was the stress of his work life that cut Edsel's life short. And part of my job is to let you know that if you let stress run roughshod over you, it could shorten your life as well. At a minimum, it could lower your quality of life.

Of course, it's not my goal here to scare you. If you're reading this book because you're feeling stressed out, I'm not here to make things worse. My goal is to help you think about ways you can give your body a fighting chance against the impacts of stress. I wouldn't be doing my job if I didn't make you aware that burnout actually does impact your physical well-being. I think too many people have the impression that burnout is merely a mental battle or a battle of emotional wellness. It certainly is that. But it's so much more. It's a physical battle as well. It's impossible to isolate the impact of a mental battle from the physical condition of the body. What we experience emotionally impacts us physically. We are holistic beings. It's all connected.

Chronic Stress and Your Body

So, keeping the fact in mind that this is not a scare tactic, let's talk about how chronic stress and burnout can impact your body. You probably aren't surprised to hear that chronic stress can damage your cardiovascular system. I think it's fairly well-known that out-of-control stress can cause you to have a heart attack. Stress and your heart function are incredibly related. In fact, that's why we often call an electrocardiogram (ECG) treadmill test of cardiovascular performance a stress test. But, familiar as we may be with that reality, we shouldn't let familiarity allow us to dismiss or downplay the risk. The truth is this: your cardiovascular system is worth protecting. Just ask your family and friends. They want your heart in tip-top shape. And, lest we think that a heart attack is the only cardiovascular risk of chronic stress, it pays to remember that the question of cardiovascular health extends beyond the health of your heart itself. Chronic stress can also make you more likely to have a stroke.[10] And just one stroke—even a nonfatal stroke— might change your life and the lives of those you love forever.

One of the biggest health impacts chronic stress can have is a reduction in the effectiveness of your immune system.[11] How big of a deal is that? Talk to anyone who struggles with a disease that compromises their immune system, and ask them how that disease impacts their daily life. As they tell you about all the precautions they must take and all the risks they manage daily, I think you'll be amazed at how much your immune system is doing for you *every minute of every day*. Let's put it this way—an immune system that is functioning well *dramatically reduces the potential of health problems in your life.* Now ask yourself: how much is that worth to you? Because one of the most profound and reliable findings of stress research over the last several decades is that chronic stress and burnout are unquestionably associated with a reduction in your immune system function.

That reduction in your immune system can translate to slower healing times, increased risk of getting sick, and even increased risk of certain types of cancer. It's a big deal. And even if you don't end up sick in some major way because your immune system isn't firing on all eight cylinders, you may be more likely to just have a sort of pesky, low-level, lingering lack of wellness that may feel like an eternal cold or a respiratory illness that just keeps hanging on. If you want to feel well, you need an immune system that is functioning at its best.

Another common outcome of chronic stress is bodily pain and inflammation.[12] Next time you're in a bookstore, pick up a medical manual and scan through the entries of illnesses that end in "-itis," like appendicitis, nephritis, or diverticulitis. These illnesses are all conditions that in some way involve bodily inflammation. And one thing we know about chronic stress is that it increases bodily inflammation. So, in concert with infection (the risk of which is potentially increased by the reduction in immune system work mentioned earlier), inflammation can be promoted by stress, causing you to be more prone to those pesky "-itis" conditions.

And inflammation can also cause all sorts of so-called phantom illness issues. Remember the guy that I talked about in the first chapter? He had lots of symptoms, but the doctors kept telling him nothing was wrong. Bodily inflammation can cause a lot of symptoms that are not likely to be given a specific diagnosis. It causes lots of aches, pains, and little weird, unfamiliar body cues that can make you feel like something is wrong with you physically. Then, if you go to the doctor and have a bunch of tests run, they're likely to tell you that they can't find the source of your symptoms. That's even scarier.

We know that one of the symptoms of stress-based inflammation can be muscle pain in your back, shoulders, and neck, as well as tension headaches. And that kind of pain can make daily life much more difficult. For many of you reading this book, muscle pain is almost a familiar friend at this point. You've dealt with it for a long time and may have almost come to terms with it. But that stiff neck is a sign of bigger problems under the hood. That inflammation is a powerful force, and it will exact even greater revenge than that muscle that feels like a clenched monkey fist in your neck.

And, in addition to what I've already talked about, we know that the following have also been connected to chronic stress or burnout:

- high cholesterol
- weight changes
- sexual dysfunction
- exhaustion
- insomnia
- pain
- muscle cramps
- nervous tics
- restlessness
- respiratory illness
- sleep problems (including difficulty falling asleep, difficulty awakening as desired, impaired sleep, etc.)
- gastrointestinal disease
- frequent indigestion
- nausea
- frequent bowel issues (constipation, diarrhea)

Note: This list is not exhaustive; it just reflects a brief flyby of what I noticed as I reviewed the academic literature on burnout.

Also, it's important to say that *you should never ignore any of these symptoms.* Just because burnout can cause these symptoms doesn't mean that it is the cause of your symptoms. And even if burnout is part of the cause, it doesn't mean that it should go unexamined or untreated. If you are experiencing any of these symptoms, you should see your physician about them.

What's a Body to Do?

Before we move on to talking about how you can win your physical battle with burnout, we should probably consider why your body reacts this way. It seems kind of counterintuitive, doesn't it? After all, we're all going to experience stress, so why would our body respond by getting sick? It's a reasonable question.

The important thing to keep in mind is something we learned about stress decades ago, and it was Dr. Hans Selye (see chapter 2) who taught us this. Dr. Selye's research indicated that our response to stress is a generalized response.[13] That means that our body responds roughly the same way to stress whether we're experiencing a physical stress (like Indiana Jones running away from the giant rolling boulder) or an emotional stress (like a financial report that must be turned in tomorrow but hasn't even been started yet). Either way, our body experiences stress as a threat to our well-being, and it gears up in roughly the same way.

When you experience a major stressor, your body gears up as though it were going to face and fight a physical threat. Your brain commands a surge of hormones like adrenaline into your system, giving you a burst of energy to fight the threat, and simultaneously starts managing a bodily attempt to keep that surge of energy from getting out of hand. Your brain, in a time of stress, begins the delicate balancing act of gearing you up to a point at which you can perform at the limits of your human capability while, at the same time, trying to keep you from gearing up to the point of physical collapse. In those moments, survival is the priority, not wellness (this is what we were talking about earlier with limp mode). Interestingly (and this is where the inflammation bit comes in), your body also gears up to deal with the possibility of being wounded. Part of your body's wound-healing routine is to cause inflammation at the site of the wound, which actually helps with healing. That's why wounds often become raised, red, and angry looking. And, since your body thinks you are being directly threatened, it releases inflammatory chemicals in your bloodstream to aid in that process.[14]

Of course, if you're being chased by a puma, all of this is very good. It's not as helpful with an emotional stressor. But so long as that emotional stressor is short-lived, it tends not to be a bad deal. Imagine, though, what happens when your body is getting used to being geared up all the time because of a chronic stressor. True, you're not geared up into full fight-or-flight mode all day long, but there is a sort of low-level activation of the stress response that stays on when you deal with chronic stress. And that activation comes with a cost. It means there are more of those inflammatory chemicals in your system than should be there. It means a bodily prioritization of survival over wellness. And it means that the pump is primed to full-on fight-or-flight mode. When you're already partially activated, it doesn't take much to push you across the line into exasperated, desperate, hit-em-with-both-barrels mode. Ever wonder why stressed people are so cranky and irritable? That's why.

We were not designed by God to live our lives in a constant state of emotional stress. That's why I believe our bodies react the way they do to ongoing emotional stressors. My atheist friends would say that we simply haven't adapted yet to the constant pressures of modern life. From an evolutionary point of view, that makes sense. As a God follower, though, I believe that there is an even bigger message here. Rather than suggesting that we just have more adapting to do for emotional stress not to have these sorts of physiological consequences, I would suggest that God did not design us to live our lives in ways that push us to the very edge of our emotional and physical limits.

In fact, your body is doing exactly what it is supposed to do when it responds to chronic stress. When you're dealing with stress overload and your system is responding to a perceived threat, your body is really being told to prioritize survival, whatever the long-term cost. And that's exactly what it will do.

Here's an example of what I mean. Imagine you take your life savings of $100,000 cash in a boat with you on a trip to a tropical island where you plan to start your retirement. But somewhere along the way, your boat springs a leak. You realize there's a hole in the boat, and you know that you're far enough from land that you will sink if you don't think of something fast. Reluctantly, you reach for some of the cash bills and roll them up into a plug for the hole. After bailing out some water you had taken on earlier, the boat begins to stabilize. And it only cost you $20,000. That money will be unrecognizable by the time you get where you're going, but you still have your life. Then another hole, and another, and another . . . by the time you reach the shore, *you're alive, but broke.* You made the best choice—after all, you're still alive and kicking—but you paid a hefty price to arrive alive. Your body is also willing to pay a hefty price to arrive alive. When you're stressed out, your body will do whatever it takes to keep you paddling safely to shore, even if it means you have to make major health compromises to plug the holes.

It's more than plugging holes, though. Your body is also trying to tell you something. Your body wants you to know that you can't go on this way. Just like a board of directors who tells a CEO that he can't keep spending money out of company reserves long-term or the company will be bankrupt, your body is warning you that you can't keep using reserve energy and expect to keep going as if nothing is wrong. The pain, the indigestion, the cold that won't go away, the insomnia, the weight changes . . . they are all trying to tell you something. They're saying, "It's too much. It's time to back off before you burn out." While the symptoms are unpleasant, you wouldn't want to turn them off. To try to get rid of the symptoms and keep living just as you are now would be something akin to putting thick black tape over the warning lights on the dash of your car so they wouldn't annoy you anymore. If you really want to fight your battle with burnout and win, you need to be prepared to tell your body this powerful little two-word phrase: *I'm listening*.

What would Edsel Ford have done if he had been really listening to what his body tried to tell him? Perhaps he would have left Ford Motor Company when he started getting stomach ulcers. It would have been painful to walk away from Ford, but he was a man in his early to midthirties with brilliance and promise; I think he would have done very well somewhere else. Maybe he would have had it out with his dad. And, for all I know, he may have tried to do that. Maybe he would have demanded a reshaping of his role at Ford. That probably would have been best for Edsel *and* for Ford Motor Company. But those sorts of things are not usually what people do when they see physical health as a side issue. They keep going, even though their body screams at them to stop. And, eventually, there's a price to pay. I grieve over what happened to Edsel, because every time I read about the guy, I'm impressed by his personal qualities. He seemed to be the kind of person who could have been an icon of great business leadership in the mid-twentieth century. His death was not only a tragedy for those who knew and loved him, it was a terrible waste of talent. Burnout always is.

What to Do?

I'm going to resist the temptation to talk about stress-reduction strategies here; we'll cover that in the next chapter. If you want to get your life back physically, you will need to pay attention to those stress-reduction techniques and take a holistic approach to reducing your stress. But for now, it's sufficient to make the point that most of us are asking our bodies to do battle with stress, knowing that we're not doing enough to even the odds and make that battle a fair fight. We're making a lot of demands on our bodies, but we're not bringing the self-discipline that is needed physically to meet those demands. If we really want to get our life back physically, we're not only going to need to reduce our stress, we're going to have to be healthier. Our body needs a fair shot at winning the stress war.

The Three Nonnegotiables

The three nonnegotiables—*diet*, *sleep*, and *exercise*—aren't original to me. In fact, I haven't reviewed a single book on stress-reduction strategies that hasn't in some way touched on all three of these. The reason you'll find them in nearly any book on stress management is that they form a sort of tripod—a three-legged stool on which your physical (and, by extension, emotional) well-being rests. When I talk to burned-out individuals, I tend to start by asking about their diet, sleep, and exercise routines. And over the years, I've learned that, for many folks, burnout paradoxically leads to *reduced* focus on these areas rather than increased focus. In fact, I'm sort of used to people telling me that diet, sleep, and exercise are such low-level concerns in comparison to what they are going through that they are almost frustrated with me for bringing them up. I get it. At this very moment, I am grappling with three academic research projects, trying to meet the deadline for this book, preparing my advanced graduate statistics students for their final, getting ready for the next academic year, and working on multiple projects at the church where I pastor. What I plan to have for lunch seems inconsequential. But it's not.

So please humor me. You may be tempted to skip past this section and avoid focusing on such mundane things as your diet, sleep patterns, and exercise routines. But they are foundational and worth your time and attention. I will try not to get too bogged down in details, but I think you'll benefit from a quick flyover of what we know about how to strengthen these three areas of physical health. And if you can make some minor changes for the better in each of these three categories, I think you'll find that you're far more successful at winning your battle with burnout than you were when you first picked up this book.

Diet

One thing we know from research is that people who are dealing with chronic stress are more likely to overeat and to eat in ways they know are unhealthy.[15] We still aren't completely sure why. One possibility is that the part of our brain that regulates impulses and considers long-term consequences is less active when we are stressed out. Probably more importantly, we know that stress eating can trigger opioid-like responses in the brain, creating pleasant feelings and reducing the pain we feel in our bodies when we're dealing with chronic stress.[16] We also know dopamine and serotonin in the brain are impacted by stress eating,[17] and so there is good reason to suspect that sometimes we eat to self-medicate our mood.

Unfortunately, stress eating is associated with two things that are very problematic—choosing foods that aren't good for you and consuming too much food. The combination of overeating and consuming bad-for-you foods puts the physiological effects of stress I mentioned earlier into a sort of hyperdrive. Our stress eating becomes its own source of bodily inflammation.[18] So instead of having one inflammation problem (the one that stress is causing), we end up with two. And while we know that stress eating can have an effect of reducing our feelings of stress in the moment, we also know that it comes with some very undesirable side effects.

First, the positive effect of stress eating on mood is extremely short-lived. To obtain that relief again, you must eat again. Second, if you are trying to watch your weight during a period of stress, you're more likely to feel shame and frustration at your own eating patterns, and that shame can start to add to your stress. Worse, you're likely to forget your previous good behavior in a moment of weakness, making you more likely to give up altogether. So if you fall away from your diet and eat a box of Twinkies because you're stressed out, not only are you likely to feel bad about yourself, you're likely to discount any progress you made up to that point and give up your goals for eating healthier. And then . . . another box of Twinkies.

I make these points because I want you to know that if you struggle with stress eating, you're not alone. And you're not crazy or pathologically undisciplined. There are real physiological reasons why eating healthy is most challenging when we're most stressed. But *it is precisely when you are most stressed that your diet needs to be as good as it can be.* Think about the bodily inflammation we talked about earlier. You can start reducing that inflammation today just by choosing a diet that fights inflammation rather than promoting it.

I won't be writing a dieting guide here. First, I'm not a dietitian. Second, there's no shortage of material out there to give you dieting guidance. Third, I tend to think that the first help you should seek in terms of diet is from your primary care physician. She knows your medical history and has a better sense than anyone else about what may or may not work for you in terms of a diet. However, here are a few pointers that may help as you begin thinking about improving your diet as part of your strategy to win your battle with burnout.

First, make *healthy* the primary goal of your diet. This is preferable to setting a goal of losing a certain number of pounds or reaching a certain body mass index (BMI). It can be helpful to track your weight and BMI, but achieving a certain number should not be the primary goal. Keep in mind that your weight and your BMI are simply two of many factors in considering whether your diet is healthy. If you make the finish line of your dietary marathon some sort of magic number, you'll be unlikely to make health a lifestyle. The goal is to make sure your body gets the nutrition it needs to be at its best. If you make healthy nutrition your goal, you won't be tempted to think you're all done with watching your diet once you arrive at a specific weight or BMI. Plenty of people have done that, and they can testify to the fact that thinking that way is a great way to gain back the weight that was lost.

Second, avoid extreme and fad diets. Psychologically, extreme diets tend to inspire a lot of enthusiasm, but people don't tend to stick with them. Maybe the enthusiasm comes from our frustration with trying other things in the past that didn't seem to work. Or maybe it's that hope in the back of our minds that this extreme new way of thinking about food will be the new leaf that we turn over that changes our lives forever. Regardless, the nature of extreme fad diets is that they tend to fizzle fast. They just don't hold up against the demands of life very well. And there's another important reason to avoid extreme and fad diets—they often tend to be very one-dimensional, focusing on a very narrow view of dietary science at the cost of a more holistic view of a healthy diet. My suggestion is that you choose a science-based, sustainable diet that is approved by your doctor. If you're going to put energy into sticking to a diet, it pays to make sure you're following a good one.

Third, monitor your progress. By this I don't mean get on the scale every half hour and obsess over your weight. I mean take reasonable steps to track your dietary choices, your weight, and your waist size. Fortunately, technology can help you do that. There are a number of great phone apps available through which you can track your meals and learn about the strengths and weaknesses of your meal and snack choices. In some of these apps, you can track your weight as well. As these apps continue to get better, guidance for your diet can become a part of what they provide, utilizing the data both from your meal choices and your success in terms of body measurements. It's been said that it's very difficult to manage what you don't measure. Diet is especially this way. Even if you're not a person who likes to track this kind of thing on your phone, some kind of diet diary is worth keeping.

Finally, if your goal is to orient your diet in a way that it is best suited to fight burnout, you'll want to investigate diets that are considered anti-inflammatory. If stress is increasing the inflammation in your body, then it would be a very desirable thing to have your diet move the needle in the opposite direction. The good news is that we know many things today about how to make anti-inflammatory choices for your diet that we didn't know years ago. With the right guidance, it is possible to have a diet that reduces inflammation and is still enjoyable and maintainable. Interestingly, one of the diets that has been identified as being generally very anti-inflammatory is the Mediterranean diet.[19] I say that's interesting because it is more than likely the kind of diet that Jesus and his disciples would have had when he was ministering on the earth. What a thought—that being Christlike in our diet could actually be one of the healthiest choices we could make to impact our stress lives. That's pretty cool.

Sleep

When I was doing research for this book, I found the topic of sleep to be especially interesting. It turns out that people who don't sleep well tend to be more burned out. And burned-out individuals tend to struggle with disturbed sleep.[20] It's a vicious cycle.

Earlier I mentioned that when I talk about diet, sleep, and exercise, people sometimes roll their eyes as though I'm mentioning strategies that are as impossible as they are obvious. Sleep is especially that way. You should see how people look at me when I say that they should be getting seven and a half restful hours of sleep each night. People tell me they think that would be lovely, but there is no possible way they could get there. Some (like medical interns or new moms) are dealing with schedules that make it difficult to get that much sleep, while others are dealing with insomnia or some health issue that makes sleep difficult. I know it sounds crazy to say that those seven and a half hours of sleep are nonnegotiable, but it's a kind of crazy I'm willing to stand by. Sure, we can all go through brief periods in our lives where we can deal with a sleep debt, but shortchanging our body on rest is never a good long-term plan.

So how do you get the sleep you need? I may be sounding like a broken record at this point, but this is yet another thing to talk to your doctor about. She can help you come up with a plan to help you achieve your sleep goals. Probably one of the things that will be on that plan is making sure your sleep hygiene is up to par. By sleep hygiene, I mean making sure that you send your body the right signals so that it understands what you are trying to do with your sleep. For instance, your bed should be devoted to sleep. Don't work on your bed if you can help it. Don't check emails or surf social media on your bed. Leave that space devoted to sleeping. If you can manage it, try to do the same for your bedroom. The more you can associate your bed and your bedroom with sleeping, the better. When you do that, your brain processes being on your bed and in your bedroom as a cue that it's time to sleep.

It's good to keep technology away from the bedroom if you can, and to limit the blue light that's emitted from electronics at least an hour before you try to go to sleep. If you can, put your phone and other notification-capable devices on some sort of do-not-disturb mode that only rings in the case of real emergencies. Limit light in your room when it's time to go to sleep. Blackout curtains are a good investment if you need to sleep during the daytime. And, as much as you can, try to develop a sleep routine that doesn't change much. Plan a bedtime and stick with it. Your body does best when your sleep falls into a rhythm. Keep in mind that *your body is trying to figure you out*. By that I mean that a lot of your physiology is designed by God to adjust to your daily patterns and optimize functions to best serve those patterns. Unfortunately, when we constantly change our sleep routine, our body struggles to establish rhythms to suit the purpose of sleeping.

Chances are very good that if you improve your sleep hygiene, your sleep amount and quality will improve. But what if it doesn't improve enough? That happens sometimes. And when that's the case, it might be a good idea to ask your doctor about pharmacological interventions to help you get the sleep you need. Hear me out on this. I know that there is often a negative knee-jerk reaction toward the idea of using medication as part of an overall sleep strategy, because none of us wants to use a medication that causes dependence or that might cause some sort of long-term problem. Those are reasonable anxiety points, and talking through the potential benefits and risks of medications with your doctor should always be part of making these sorts of decisions. But it might help to know in this context that often very low-dose, low-risk medication strategies can be implemented that can make a big difference in helping you get the sleep you need. Sleep is a foundation for your physical and emotional health, so deciding to be content with getting less sleep than you need is probably not the best course of action. It pays to consider all your options.

Exercise

It might seem weird to propose that exercise (an activity that actually puts your body under some stress) is a good strategy to battle burnout and chronic stress. But the right kinds of exercise tend to be good stress for your body. Think about the fact that in fight-or-flight mode, your body is really gearing up to physically escape from a threat. So your body is gearing up for exercise. When you don't exercise, then your physiology is, in a sense, all geared up with no place to go.[21] But when we choose to do aerobic exercise in reasonable amounts, we can use the response our body has mounted, force a period of relaxation (that tends to follow elective exercise), and experience the endorphin and opioid-like chemical release in the brain that also helps in the process of resetting from stress.

Exercise, like diet, unfortunately is an area of life in which people often have the best of intentions but the worst of follow-through. If the gyms in our communities were frequented by everyone who had memberships, there wouldn't be enough space or equipment to handle the crowds. Gyms tend to operate on the understanding that a sizable percentage of people who pay for memberships won't show up at all. And what's funny is that many of those individuals will renew their membership when it comes due, simply because in their heart, they really do intend to use it. *As soon as life slows down,* they think, *I'll be there.* But life rarely slows down. You'll have to make time for exercise.

There's some really good news, though. If you are a person who needs to make time for exercise, let me put you at ease—the kind of exercise you need to do if you want to battle burnout doesn't have to happen at the gym, and it doesn't have to absorb a lot of your time. We know from research that you don't have to do the kinds of exercises that body builders do (lifting heavy weights, bench-pressing large objects, etc.) to fight stress.[22] In fact, one school of thought holds that medium-intensity aerobic exercise seems to help the most. Something as simple as taking a walk around your neighborhood several times a week counts as the kind of exercise that can really pay dividends in helping you deal with stress. Of course, there's nothing wrong with building muscle, so if you want to do the intense stuff, go for it. Just make sure that you're not neglecting the medium-intensity exercise that can really help you fight a good fight in terms of bodily stress.

The best way to get started is to talk to your doctor. Ask her to help you put together a basic weekly exercise plan that fits with your own physical abilities and goals. Then, do your best to make time for that exercise. It will be worth it in the end. You might be interested to know that in some research, exercise has been as effective as antidepressant medication in fighting depression.[23] I'm not suggesting that a person taking antidepressants should get rid of them in favor of exercise. In fact, I am a fan of good psychopharmacological intervention for depression. But it is interesting that exercise can be so powerful that it can rival some of the best medications we have for fighting depression. You might be surprised what implementing a realistic exercise regimen in your life would do for your mood and overall well-being.

A Biblical Perspective

Before we close out this chapter, I want to take a moment and remind those of us who are believers in Jesus Christ that how we address stress in our bodies is a consideration with sacred implications. The Bible tells us that our bodies are the temple of the Holy Spirit, and once we give our lives to God, our bodies belong to God as well. The reason I mention this is because it can be easy for us to look at the physiological costs of stress as a sort of cost of doing business in life. We can really be prone to think of the impact of stress on our body as a price we're willing to pay, acting as though it's no big deal if we eventually do have a heart attack or stroke because of stress. Our motto can easily become *It is what it is*. But the Bible says that for those of us who are believers, we are stewards of our bodies, not the owners. So since God has given us these bodies, it's our job as good stewards to maintain them well and get the most out of them. And doing that means we need to be serious about combating stress at the physical level.

Earlier I talked about the prophet Elijah and his bout with burnout. I would make the case in this context that it is important that when the angel ministered to Elijah, the prophet was made to eat twice, sleep, and take a very long walk. That's diet, sleep, and exercise. The formula hasn't changed much over the past several thousand years.

CHAPTER 3
Group Discussion Questions

1. We talked about a lot of different physical aspects of life that stress can impact. To whatever extent you're comfortable, perhaps you could share with the group how you think stress may impact you physically.

2. How does the physical nature of stress influence the way you view this passage of Scripture? 1 Corinthians 6:19–20 (ESV): "Or do you not know that your body is a temple of the Holy Spirit within you, whom you have from God? You are not your own, for you were bought with a price. So glorify God in your body."

3. To the extent that you're comfortable, share with the group what your experience has been with exercise and physical activity and how they've impacted your stress life for the better or worse.

4. To the extent that you're comfortable, talk about your journey with nutrition. What have you experienced when it comes to trying to eat healthy?

5. What have you dealt with in terms of sleep health? Have you tried sleep hygiene strategies to get good sleep? What has been your experience with those?

Getting Your Life Back Emotionally

Mike Wallace was a titan of investigative journalism. He was known for his hard-hitting, unflinching style in interviews, which caused even some of the most rock-ribbed guests to experience something called "Mike fright."[1] In fact, there was a time when some quipped that the four most dreaded words among those in the public eye were "Mike Wallace is here."[2] Wallace was an example of a person who handled stress in ways that few of the rest of us can. There are few things as stressful as having to direct mental traffic at the speed of a high-stakes conversation that is being filmed for millions of viewers to watch. People in journalism and PR know the power that single interviews—even single quotes from an interview—can have over a journalist's career. Yet Mike Wallace fearlessly faced the biggest names out there. He was an example of the kind of guy who faces the biggest stressors in life and doesn't flinch.

You may remember that one of my earlier points is that people like Mike Wallace have developed a sort of adaptation to the stresses of life that makes them look almost superhuman. But you'll also remember that I made the point that, even for people who live their lives in a state of very high adaptation, there will come a time when they'll run out of energy if they're not careful. And that happened to Mike Wallace. In 1984, Wallace was dealing with the pain of an impending divorce and a lawsuit that called his investigative integrity into question.[3] Not willing to put his career on hold to deal with these issues, he scheduled his interviews at night and attended court during the day.[4] Court was a nightmare. Although Mike eventually came out on top of that legal battle, some of the testimony that came out in that trial was very difficult to sit through. Some witnesses suggested that he cared more about money than accuracy in reporting. And, worse still, some witnesses suggested that he was more interested in ratings than national stability.

Who knows what the straw was that broke the camel's back? Maybe it was the divorce and being displaced from the home where he had lived for decades. Maybe it was the court case. Or maybe it was the insane schedule he was trying to keep. Maybe it was the combination of all those things. Regardless, one night he hit a wall. He would later say that he had the feeling that he just "had to get out of here."[5] And "here" didn't mean his apartment. It meant life. In that moment of desperation, he wrote a suicide note, consumed a bottle of sleeping pills, and fell asleep, intending not to wake up. Had it not been for the new lady in his life who found him in that condition, Mike Wallace would have quietly passed away, another public figure lost to suicide.[6]

It would be many years before Wallace would be ready to talk on record about that dark night in 1984. And when he did, he would blame a bout with depression for his near-fatal overdose. [7] And that's appropriate. I'm sure he was depressed. Burnout is a path to full-on depression. However, I would make the case that what caused Mike Wallace to crash in such a profound way was a prototypical case of burnout brought on by chronic stress. The emotional fallout was entirely predictable if you look at it that way. Burnout (and, more specifically, the chronic stress that causes burnout) impacts the ways in which our brains function, making depression and anxiety much more likely to take hold.[8]

By the way, Mike Wallace is just one of many examples. During a season when Walt Disney was having break-through success with animated films, he hit a point of burnout as well. In those days, he recalled, the unrelenting burden of his job pushed him to a place where he struggled to talk on the phone without weeping. "I was an emotional flap . . ." he recalled.[9] F. Scott Fitzgerald, the author of *The Great Gatsby*, had a season of burnout that was so life-upending that he wrote an essay about the experience, which he called "The Crack-Up," later included in a book.[10]

The famous comedian Charlie Chaplin, when going through a painful divorce and dealing with the stresses of fame and the demands of comedic creativity, tried to take his own life by jumping out a two-story window. In a news interview he gave shortly after, Chaplin made the remark, "My ability as an actor is very aerial, very frail—you don't know whether the spark will die."[11] Chaplin's remark is relevant to what we're discussing here. Remember that bell curve of stress we talked about in chapter 1? When you're at the sweet spot of that bell curve, your spark will be bright and reliable. You'll be creative, flexible, able to remember things, productive, and emotionally in a good place. When you've pushed yourself much too far, that spark will be dim and, as Chaplin said, "very aerial, very frail."

Let's ask the obvious question. How on earth does a person like Mike Wallace become suicidal? We might expect a suicide attempt from a person who is emotionally unstable or weak, but not from a guy whose emotional strength was his personal trademark. How does someone who is typically an emotional rock become emotional Jell-O? One word—*exhaustion*. Managing your emotions is one of the most energy-costly things your brain does. And it is possible to run out of that energy. When you do, you may be shocked to find how unmanaged your emotions can become.

Here's an example. Think of the most reliable driver you know. Chances are you'd have no issue climbing into the passenger seat and letting them take you on a long drive. You'd feel safe. In fact, you might even be comfortable falling asleep, knowing that a reliable driver was at the wheel. Now imagine that your reliable motorist friend begins to tell you that they are feeling sleepy. You see their head bobbing a bit, and it seems like they are right on that paper-thin line between awake and asleep. How would you feel about being in the passenger seat now? No matter how reliable the driver, you're not likely to put your life in the hands of someone who is fighting off exhaustion. You know better than that. You know that once that person falls asleep, all their driving skill becomes irrelevant and you're going for a wild ride.

It's a similarly wild ride when a person who is normally an emotion-management pro runs out of steam and begins to shut down. In fact, if you deal with a true case of burnout and become emotionally depleted, you may find yourself acting completely out of character, just as it was out of character for Mike Wallace to pen a suicide note and down a bottle of pills. That wasn't the Mike his friends knew and loved. Remember our super rats from chapter 2? There was a point at which, no matter how well the rats had adapted along the way, they simply ran out of energy to meet the demands of their environment, and they collapsed (the rats died). There's a similar sort of collapse that happens to us when we imagine we will always be able to adapt to whatever emotional burdens or challenges life throws at us. At some point, the energy tank will be empty, we'll face one emotional demand too many, and, while it's unlikely to be fatal, there will be a sort of internal collapse. Emotionally, it will be too much to handle.

The Face of Emotional Exhaustion

I saw this firsthand years ago with my own father, who gave permission to share his story. My dad is the senior pastor of one of the most innovative, forward-moving churches in the United States. Under his leadership, the church grew from around 300 people in weekly attendance to its current weekly attendance of around 7,000. Mark Hoover is known for his pioneering leadership style and, perhaps more than anything else, his emotional stability. My dad epitomizes Kipling's true measure of a man in his poem "If" as one who can "can keep your head when all about you are losing theirs and blaming it on you." I watched my dad shepherd the church through two major initiatives—the first being a major relocation and building project, and the second being a complete shift of ministry focus and style. In both cases I watched my dad deal with the stress of risking everything for the sake of a God-given vision. And I watched him deal with personal attacks from those who didn't share that vision. But in all that time, my dad remained his stable, wise self. If there were a picture in the encyclopedia next to emotional stability, I would have nominated my dad's photograph for that slot.

But emotional exhaustion can happen to anyone. That goes even for those who have weathered so many storms that they seem to be invincible. And I've noticed there always seems to be a last straw. It doesn't have to be a catastrophe that brings about the emotional apocalypse. It just has to be one thing too many: a demand for emotional energy—no matter how small—after the emotional energy is all gone. For my dad, I would say the last straw was the departure of a staff member and friend with whom he'd weathered much of the storm of the ideological transition of the church. The year was 2010, and I had just joined the church staff as associate pastor. Having lost the key member of our staff I just mentioned, my dad and I were sifting through hundreds of résumés, looking for a replacement. And we were realizing how difficult it would be to replace the unique individual God had placed in that role for the previous several years.

Maybe it was the stress of having a great friend and ministry partner leave and move to another ministry. Maybe it was the compounded stress of trying to find a new person to fill the role that was now vacant. Maybe it was the years of pioneering stress of leading a ministry through challenging days and sleepless nights. I would wager it was all of the above and more. But I saw it finally take its toll one day in our senior staff meeting. I noticed that my dad seemed off. He just wasn't his normal self. I asked if I could stay for a few minutes afterward to discuss something with him, and he nodded. After everyone else had left, I tried to converse with him about something minor and noticed that he wasn't making eye contact with me. Instead he was staring into space with a look on his face I'd never seen before. I asked him a direct question and got no answer. I knew something was wrong.

Later that day, I would receive nearly simultaneous phone calls from my mom and from the executive pastor of our church, letting me know that my dad was not doing well. They wanted me to know they were trying to get him some help. Meanwhile, as a twenty-nine-year-old newly minted pastor, I was to step in and preach on the weekends in my dad's place. We were all scrambling to figure out what to do. And the one person I would normally have asked for advice was falling apart emotionally.

At that time, my dad was convinced he was dying (which is not an uncommon thing among people having nervous breakdowns). He was dealing with intense feelings of personal failure despite his clear track record of success, and he was an emotional basket case. He was toggling between anxious moments of pacing and fretting and weepy moments of depression and sadness. Even though my dad loves music, he didn't want to hear any. Even though he typically enjoys watching an old sitcom on TV or watching a documentary, he didn't want any TV screens on. He didn't really trust anyone except my mom in his worst moments, and he became very dependent on her in a way that was not at all normal for him. It was almost like he was a completely different person.

And that's what emotional exhaustion looks like. When you run out of energy to regulate yourself emotionally, you lose a lot of who you normally are. For instance, two of the most energy-taxing things your brain does in terms of emotions is help you manage your anxieties and regulate your motivations. It takes real energy for your brain to decide how to deal with the anxious reactions you have to the stressors and challenges of life. And it takes energy to stay motivated to do the things you have to do and to keep some resilience going when you encounter setbacks. But when you run out of energy to manage those two things, you can face new and unfamiliar battles with anxiety and depression. My dad was dealing with that. Several weeks into his battle with burnout, I would wager he could easily have been diagnosed with major depressive disorder *and* generalized anxiety disorder. In my opinion, the source of those disorders in that season of his life was an empty emotional gas tank. He just had no energy left to fight the daily battles with emotional stress that he had fought so well before.

Of course, emotional exhaustion will do more than make you anxious and depressed. It will leave you feeling emotionally numb at moments and then hypersensitive at others. You'll notice that you have a shorter fuse than you used to, because that fuse is made of—you guessed it—emotional energy. The less emotional energy you have, the shorter your fuse. You'll find yourself stressing about and prioritizing unimportant things and procrastinating when it comes to things that really need your attention.

You may find yourself giving in to temptation in areas where you would usually exercise self-control, because self-control requires a lot of emotional energy. You'll probably start seeing yourself in a negative light, feeling like a failure at some moments, and feeling a sort of fuzzy, indistinct sense of shame at other moments. As you can imagine, the reason for this is because self-confidence requires emotional energy.

The list goes on. Trust requires emotional energy, so you may struggle to know who you can listen to and believe. Self-preservation requires emotional energy, so you may find yourself less likely to prioritize self-care routines. And even your relationship with God requires some emotional energy, so you may feel like, at a time when you need to feel God more than ever, you feel his presence less.

You Can (and Will) Recover

On an airplane headed to get help for his emotional distress, my dad looked at my mom and said, "I don't know if I can ever go back." I think that's a feeling nearly everyone who deals with a severe case of burnout can identify with. When you have a breakdown because of stress, it's easy to think that you'll never recover and be the best version of yourself again. But take it from someone who has seen it happen repeatedly with those I've counseled over the years—you can recover, and chances are, you'll be better than ever.

My dad did spend several weeks away from NewSpring Church getting help for his emotional distress. And, when he came back to his role at NewSpring, he did have to ease into the workload somewhat gradually. But anyone who has witnessed his thirteen years of ministry since will tell you that his best season of ministry has been the time *after* his battle with burnout. I feel confident that your best days are ahead as well.

The key thing to realize here is that *your emotional energy is a precious resource.* When that well runs dry, your priority needs to be finding ways to replenish that energy. Then, your next priority needs to be finding ways to avoid depleting yourself this way in the future. If you can do those two things, you'll be well on your way to winning your burnout battle.

Rest Like You Stress

Up until now, I've been making the case that your energy (both physical and emotional) is a finite, exhaustible resource. Now the good news—it is also a *renewable* resource. You're not stuck with a fixed level of energy to face the challenges of life; you can actually refill your energy tank. The way to do that is with the *strategic use of rest*. In short, if you want a balanced, healthy life, you need to *rest like you stress*. Whatever energy you require, you must replenish. And that replenishing comes from allowing yourself to recover by disconnecting from the grind.

By the way, when I say the strategic use of rest, I mean that *how you rest should not be an afterthought*. Here's what I mean by that: today I went to the gym to work out. No need to applaud. I hadn't been there for months. I returned to the gym in an effort to return to a more healthy lifestyle. That's part of it. The other part is that I find spending time at the gym to be a tremendous help for my writing on stress. All over the gym you see examples of how you can use stress to your advantage: to build strength, rather than to deplete it. Today I overheard a personal trainer walking a new client through the workout routine he had prescribed to them. He explained that they would be taking a three-minute rest between high-intensity sets.

"Three minutes?" the client interrupted. "I don't need three minutes between sets. Give me thirty seconds, and I'll be good to go."

I was also surprised to hear three minutes prescribed. I didn't even know that there was such a thing as timing your rest periods. Usually when I worked out with a trainer years ago, rests were treated as a necessary evil between sets. They were something you just did. No parameters, no guidelines—it was assumed you knew how to rest instinctively.

Having heard this discussion at the gym, I was curious. So when I got home, I did what college professors do best. I consulted academic research sources. I was amazed to find out that the research really does support the idea that *how you rest* can be extremely important when it comes to the effectiveness of your workout.[12] And, more relevant to our current discussion about burnout and handling stress, how body builders rest actually has a lot to do with how much they can lift and how many reps they can do. So we could extract from that the idea that how you rest impacts how much life stress you can handle before your body and brain force a hard stop.

The other thing I noticed in the research is that the longest rest periods were needed for those who were trying to lift weight at the high end of their capabilities.[13] A person capable of bench pressing three hundred pounds doesn't need a three-minute rest period between light sets of weight lifting. On the other hand, if they max out their capacity and lift the full three hundred pounds, they will need those long rest periods between sets to get their optimum level of performance.

I am assuming you are reading this book because either you or someone you love is pushing themselves to the limits of their abilities. If that's the case, *resting like you stress* is crucial. And, like the example of resting between workout sets that we've used here, chances are the rest periods that you will need will be longer than you might expect. But the exercise research shows that when people rest strategically, their endurance and reliability of performance increases. That's what we need when it comes to building up emotional performance strength to battle burnout.

Three Kinds of Rest

I've already emphasized one thing you can do to improve your rest regimen, and that's getting an adequate amount of and better quality sleep. Now I want to expand our thinking about rest beyond our nightly sleep routines. To support our key idea that you need to *rest like you stress*, we'll think of anything that allows you to *unplug from your stress burden* and *replenish your energy supply* as a way of resting.

The idea of unplugging from your stress load may seem impossible right now. Chances are, you're reading this book because you are going through a particularly stressful time. And you're probably thinking that, while the idea of taking a break from your burdens is very pleasant, it's simply not feasible. But for all those who say that break taking isn't an option, I have to force a bit of a reality check: the truth is that you will be taking a break at some point. You can take a break now, strategically, on your terms, or life will force a break on you later, and it won't be as manageable.

Put another way, you can either unplug and recharge, or you can burn out. But that really shouldn't surprise us. We're used to this. Every night before I go to bed, I plug in my smartphone so that it can recharge. I don't do that because I find recharging my phone to be a great joy in my life or because I find it pleasurable to do so. I plug my phone in because it's an opportunity to address the limited energy of that device on my own schedule, on my own terms, and in a way that causes the least disruption to my life. If I decided not to recharge the phone, I would still endure a disruption later on . . . when the phone runs out of energy completely. It just will be less convenient and less predictable.

That's why I'm making the point that strategic rest—strategic unplugging and recharging—is the way to take control of your stress life. It's the way to predictably ensure that your emotional well-being can stay strong even when you're having to deal with heavy stress burdens. Let me encourage you to resist the temptation to tell yourself that you can't afford to unplug. Just remind yourself that *recharging isn't an option*. Downtime will happen. The options are *how* and *when* you will recharge.

Just as we talked about three major components of physical wellness that can be used to fight back against burnout—diet, sleep, and exercise—we will now look at three components of strategic rest that can help you refill your tank with emotional energy—break taking, energizing activities, and relaxation techniques.

Break Taking

When it comes to strategic rest, break taking may well be the most powerfully impactful thing you can do, and it also may be the one you're least likely to feel comfortable using. It can be a bit anxiety provoking to think of stepping away from your situation, however briefly, because the more stressed out you become the more likely you are to think that without your constant efforts, the world will fall apart. I don't say that mockingly. I understand that your presence and active problem-solving in whatever situation you are facing right now is making a big difference.

For instance, I know of several individuals right now who are dealing with burnout because of having to care for an aging parent or a terminally ill spouse. Of course they are making a *huge* difference by being there and providing care. And, in my opinion, they are living out the love of Jesus by providing that care and loving support. But remember what we said above—if they are not taking strategic breaks to recharge, life will force them to take a break at some point.

Short Breaks

Here's a key thought that may help you embrace the idea of strategic break taking: *brief breaks count.* Sometimes we think of breaks as needing to be long, drawn-out affairs, like a two-week beach vacation or a sabbatical. I'm all for sabbaticals and beach vacations (perhaps both at the same time), but you can be a pro at break taking without going to such extremes. In fact, very short breaks (sometimes called "microbreaks") can be effective.

In one study, surgeons were given the opportunity to try taking microbreaks during long surgical procedures. They were able, in addition to taking a moment to recover from the moment-to-moment stress of the procedure, to do some basic physical stretches and exercises that were doable in a sterile surgical environment. The results were very encouraging. Over 34 percent of the surgeons said their mental focus improved from simply doing the microbreak routine. Add that to the over 53 percent who said their mental focus was the same as usual, and you get over 87 percent of surgeons saying their focus was as strong as normal or better when they were taking these microbreaks. Here's an even more encouraging statistic: over 57 percent of surgeons said their physical performance (which presumably would be related to the tension they felt in their bodies and their brain/hand/eye coordination) was improved as a result of the microbreaks.[14]

My point here is that if you're thinking *my situation won't allow me to take long breaks,* that shouldn't keep you from experiencing the powerful benefit strategic rest can provide. Take the breaks you can, in the way that you can; it will make a difference. There are lots of different ways to structure a meaningful, energizing break. Do what works for you. In my own break-taking practice, I've found three important elements of a great break: focus shifting, relaxation, and gratitude. Here I'll go through a quick routine that you can use to practice all three. Later I'll share several other techniques you can use for relaxation. For now, just look at this little break script and watch for the three components I just mentioned.

Sitting Break in Quiet Room— Nonreligious Version

It's break time. Time to let go of what you were thinking about as you walked into this room and sat down. Think for a moment about what was stressing you out moments ago. Imagine that you put that problem into a cardboard box that is tied to several large, colorful balloons. Soon enough, the balloons lift that box into the air, and the wind carries it gently away. You watch as it fades from view. It will come back later; right now, that problem is at a distance. You are here now, and it's a good time to pay attention to what is undeniably here as well. Your breath is here. Feel your breath as it slowly goes out and in. If you can, take a full breath in through your nose, and let it out slowly through your mouth, as if through a drinking straw. Feel your body calming as you slowly and gently exhale. If you are able, gently turn your neck from side to side, then shrug and rotate your shoulders gently. Finally, lift your hands in the air and stretch as if you just woke up and were anticipating a great new day. Now, as you sit back in a comfortable position, feel the muscles you were just stretching as they settle and become relaxed. Think for a moment about a pleasant place in your childhood or a pleasant memory. Imagine the sights, sounds, smells, and textures of that place. For a moment, allow yourself to remember all you can about that pleasant moment or place. Then, as you mentally rest in that place for a moment, ask yourself, *What am I thankful for? Who or what in my life can I authentically celebrate at this moment as being a blessing?* Rest for a moment in that gratitude. Now, as you prepare to end your break, take three deep breaths and begin to allow that balloon box to gently sail back toward you. The box is heavy, but breaks like this will help you as you carry the load. And, as you carry the box from this room, also remember to carry the gratitude you practiced earlier with you as well. It will help lighten the load of whatever happens to be in the box.

Sitting Break in Quiet Room— Christian Version

It's break time. Time to let go of what you were thinking about as you walked into this room and sat down. Think for a moment about what was stressing you out moments ago. Imagine that we put that problem into a cardboard box, which you carry to Jesus and then ask him to hold for you as you take this break. In fact, take a moment and tell Jesus about what you put in the box. He is here in this room with you. The box is imaginary, but you are real, Jesus is real, and the problem is real. Tell him what's in the box. Ask him to hold it. He will. And, as the problem is no longer in your hands, you can take a moment to be fully present. You are here now, and it's a good time to pay attention to what is undeniably here as well. The Holy Spirit is here with you. As a believer in Jesus, you can rest in the knowledge that God himself is with you through his Holy Spirit. Guess what one of the Holy Spirit's biggest jobs is? To comfort you. Take a moment and let it settle in that the God of the universe wants to comfort you in this moment. God is here with you. Also, your breath is here. It's good to take a moment and get connected with what's going on in your body, and your breath will help you do that. Feel your breath as it slowly goes out and in. If you can, take a full breath in through your nose, and let it out slowly through your mouth, as if through a drinking straw. Feel your body calming as you slowly and gently exhale. If you are able, gently turn your neck from side to side, then shrug and rotate your shoulders gently. Finally, lift your hands in the air and stretch as if you just woke up and were anticipating a great new day. Now, as you sit back in a comfortable position, feel the muscles you were just stretching as they settle and become relaxed. Think for a moment about a pleasant place in your childhood or a pleasant memory. Imagine the sights, sounds, smells, and textures of that place. For a moment, allow yourself to remember all you can about that pleasant moment or place. Then, as you mentally rest in that place for a moment, ask yourself, *What am I thankful for? Who or what in my life can I authentically celebrate at this moment as being a blessing?* Rest for a moment in that gratitude. Remember that God has been holding your box for you. Before you approach him about what's in the box, tell him what you were just feeling thankful for. He's promised to

give you peace if you'll talk to him about two things: what's
in the box and what you're thankful for. Afterward, as you approach Jesus and the box you gave him, ask him for guidance
about what you should take back from the box and what you
should leave with him. You weren't meant to carry this all
yourself. Now, as you prepare to end your break, take three
deep breaths, think of something to smile about, and remind
yourself that God is with you.

If doing this sort of routine kind of creeps you out, then don't
throw the baby out with the bathwater. Take a short break and
drink a bottle of water. Take a short break and listen to one of your
favorite songs on your smartphone. Pull up an abstract painting on
your smartphone and allow yourself to enjoy and think through
the colors, textures, and patterns (Van Gogh is one of my favorites).
If you find smells particularly relaxing, go to the local candle shop
and buy a votive with a scent you love and take in that scent during
a break. If you are a very tactile person, go to the local fabric store
and buy a small piece of fabric that has a texture you like. As you
take a break, rub your fingers over the texture of the fabric as a
calming aid. Any of these things can work, and there are a million
ways to take breaks that I haven't mentioned. But unless you decide
to give strategic breaks a try, you won't know what works for you.
Try a one-week challenge and plan on taking three microbreaks
a day for those seven days. If you get nothing out of it, then fine.
But my hunch is you'll find it makes a big enough difference that
you'll become a microbreak believer.

Longer Breaks

While brief breaks do count, sometimes you need a longer
break. In chapter 2, we talked about super rats. I mentioned that
when a super rat that is being stored in the coldest refrigerator

begins to run out of energy, it will die unless it is removed completely from the cold. That means that it will still die even if it is moved to the less-cold refrigerator. What does that mean in the real world? It means that there is a time when a long break is necessary. I would make the case that the length of the break should correspond to the severity of the stress crisis. Earlier I talked about my dad's experience of going through an emotional and physical breakdown. The time that he spent completely unplugged from his normal stress burden was between five and six weeks. To some, that might seem like a lengthy break. But the severity of the crisis called for more than a few days off.

If you are reading this book because you or someone you love is going through a profound stress crisis where there is a sort of full-on emotional breakdown happening, a complete break from work and stressful situations may be necessary (to the extent that it's possible). And, I would quickly add that a break like that needs to include seeking help from therapists and physicians who can help chart a trajectory toward wellness. Here's a word of caution: be careful not to ruin the effectiveness of a long break by sneaking work or other stress into your season of recharging. If you're invested in not making your long break longer than it needs to be, keep it a work-sterile environment as much as you can.

Also, don't confuse a change in location with taking a break. I know some people who think they're taking a break when they go on a five-night cruise and have excursions planned every day they're gone. Once they're done touring, scuba diving, Mayan ruins photographing, and wine tasting, they're surprised that they aren't deeply relaxed from their time off. A break should be a break. Trading one type of stress for another will mess up whatever good the break might do for you. I'm not suggesting you should sit still on a park bench and twiddle your thumbs all day when you take strategic time off. That would drive me nuts. What I am saying is that whatever activities you do engage in should be energizing activities. What are those, you ask? Read on, my friend.

Energizing Activities

Resting is not just about what you choose not to do. It's also about what you choose to do. If this is a book you can mark in, take a pencil out and write in different activities in your life that belong in each band of the graph below. What are activities that are intensely draining, draining, challenging, energizing, or intensely energizing for you? When you start plotting them out, you'll start to realize that not all *doing* is equal. Some things you do can be intensely energy giving, while other things you do can be intensely energy zapping. It's those things that are in the energizing or intensely energizing categories that we're talking about in this section. Those are the things that you can do that count as strategic rest.

Before you fill out the chart, let me clarify something. In the early days of this chart, I used to tell people they couldn't put work activities in the energizing or intensely energizing areas. I'm not sure why I did that. I think it was because I assumed that strategic rest should not ever include work, and I was also convinced that many of the burned-out people I was helping were workaholics. At the time, I thought that part of my job was to remind people that if they found their job to be addicting, they needed to recover from that drug.

Now I've changed my mind. It doesn't make you a workaholic if you find parts of your job intensely energizing. It just means that you've probably found an occupation that is an excellent fit for you. So feel free to put both work and nonwork activities on your chart. However, if you find that your entire chart is full of work activities, and there are no other activities listed, you may want to consider whether your life is becoming a bit one-dimensional. No matter how great your work is, there should be more to life than your job. Okay, the disclaimers are done. Fill out the chart and see where you stand.

This is where you can't compare notes with others. What is intensely energizing for someone else might be draining for you.

Figure 4.1

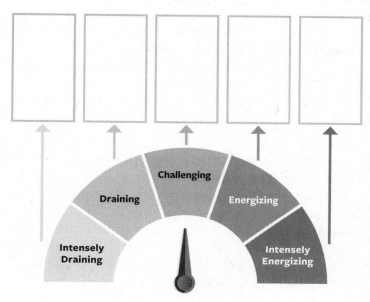

Knowing what should go in these boxes is a matter of personal awareness and trial and error. For instance, knowing that I like working with my hands and trying a lot of different hobbies led me to find that woodworking is very energizing for me. You might find woodworking to be frustrating or boring. On the other hand, there are people in my life who love the sport of golf. I really want to love it, too. I just don't. While golf is an energizing activity for them, it is somewhere between the low end of challenging and the high end of draining on this chart for me. If I do play golf, it's because I enjoy hanging out with the people who invite me. But I know going in that it's not going to recharge my batteries. So if someone tells you they have the perfect hobby to help you de-stress, smile and nod politely, but keep in mind that nobody but you and perhaps the people closest to you will know what really energizes you. Don't be surprised if you try someone else's foolproof relaxation activity and it makes you more tense. This is a personal thing. It requires a personal solution.

Here's how to use this graph. I would encourage you to see if it is possible to delegate or discontinue activities that appear in the intensely draining category when it is reasonable to do so. Of course, it would not be appropriate to discontinue taking care of a loved one, even if it is intensely draining. In cases like that, however, it would be worthwhile to see what could be done to change the tasks of caring for that loved one such that it might migrate to the draining or challenging parts of the chart. We really don't want to leave any activity in the intensely draining category for long. When you're working and expending energy, it's okay to have the needle point toward challenging quite a bit and draining from time to time. But we also would want to see that needle bouncing up into the energizing zones just as often. However, when you're trying to rest, that needle should be hanging out in the energizing to intensely energizing zones. If it's bouncing around in the challenging and draining zones, you're not resting.

Relaxation Techniques

Before ending this chapter on strategic rest as a way of recharging emotionally, I'd like to mention one other rest strategy that gets a lot of attention these days. You're unlikely to read any book on stress or burnout without seeing something about relaxation techniques. And there are a ton of relaxation techniques. You may have heard of the use of yoga, mindfulness, or meditation as ways of reducing stress. Alternatively, you may have read about progressive relaxation, physical therapy, or even massage as strategic relaxation strategies. So what about those?

In general, these relaxation techniques work very well.[15] The reason they work is that there is a two-way conversation happening between your brain and the rest of your body about how stressed you are or should be.[16] When your brain experiences stress, it sends signals to the body that then gear the body up to be stressed. When the brain then polls the body and finds it to be stressed out (muscle tension, shallow breathing, etc.), it gets even more stressed out and sends even stronger stress signals to the body. It's like a feedback loop.

There are two ways to stop the loop. Either you can calm down your brain and convince it to stop freaking your body out, or you can calm down your body in an effort to send calming signals to your brain. Some relaxation techniques are aimed at calming your body down, which is arguably easier than trying to convince your brain to chill out. Examples of these techniques would be breathing exercises and progressive relaxation. Other practices like yoga or mindfulness meditation are aimed at calming both the brain and the rest of the body.

The good news is that, generally speaking, most mainline relaxation techniques do a great job of reducing overall stress. So don't be afraid to try relaxation techniques, so long as you learn about them from reputable sources and your physician gives them the okay. For Christians, it pays to know that in the yoga and mindfulness communities, there are a lot of folks who embed Eastern mysticism into their practice, which sometimes conflicts strongly with Christian beliefs. The good news is that these Christianity-incompatible beliefs are not necessary in order to do and benefit from yoga or mindfulness exercises. The even better news is that, in the past several years, several Christian-oriented mindfulness and yoga models have emerged, and I, for one, am very thankful for the opportunity to try them out.

A Biblical Perspective

If you grew up going to Sunday school as I did, you probably are familiar with the story of Jesus feeding at least 5,000 people with a little boy's sack lunch. You probably remember that the reason Jesus had to feed these people is that the disciples were with Jesus in a remote place where no vendors were present to sell food. So why was Jesus in a remote place? Back up a few verses and you'll see:

> The apostles returned to Jesus from their ministry tour and told him all they had done and taught. Then Jesus said, "Let's go off by ourselves to a quiet place and rest awhile." He said this because there were so many people coming and going that Jesus and his apostles didn't even have time to eat. So they left by boat for a quiet place, where they could be alone.
>
> Mark 6:30–32

The ministry tour mentioned here was Jesus's sending of the disciples out to minister in groups of two. Because of the divine power that was given to them, their ability to teach, heal people, and cast out evil spirits had sparked a lot of interest. As they returned and reconvened, so did the crowds that had gathered during their season of independent ministry. They had been ministering apart from each other. Imagine the electricity as they were now together as a group, ministering with this new power they had been given by God. But in the middle of this huge surge of ministry and focusing of God's power in one area, Jesus unexpectedly said they needed to step away as a group. Why? For the purpose of *resting intentionally*. It's easy to say we don't have time to rest. Jesus's disciples didn't even have an "opportune time" to eat, but he encouraged them to reprioritize and *make time* for rest.[17] That's strategic rest. That's what we're talking about.

That's the reason the crowds ended up in such a remote place. It's because they followed Jesus, who was intending to take his disciples to a "quiet place, where they could be alone" (Mark 6:32). The lesson here is that there is a need in every one of our hearts to find a quiet place where we can be alone with God for the purpose of intentionally resting. A place where we can "be still and know" (Psalm 46:10) that he has "overcome the world" (John 16:33) and the situations we face in it. A place where we can remember that "apart from [him we] can do nothing" (John 15:5). And a place where, in our stillness, we can "see the salvation of the LORD, which He will accomplish for you . . ." (Exodus 14:13 NKJV).

That's where we win our battle with burnout emotionally. We win it in our quiet places, in taking breaks, in activities where our passion recharges our batteries, and in our ability to relax, knowing that God can manage what we cannot.

CHAPTER 4
Group Discussion Questions

1. Have you experienced others downplaying emotion, implying it is an unimportant part of life? What is your opinion of how important emotion is in life?

2. What has your experience been with break taking? Has it helped your stress? What do you do on breaks to recharge?

3. What kind of restful activities work for you, and how do you manage to prioritize those activities?

4. Do you think you ever truly relax? If so, what is your strategy for relaxation? Does it work well? Is there a downside?

5. Based on your understanding of Scripture, how important do you think our emotional health is to God?

Getting Your Life Back Relationally

Dear burned-out spouse,

I don't know how to help you. I've watched you take on the world for so long now, and I have mixed feelings. I'm proud of what you are doing and what you've accomplished. But I also am so worried about what all of this is doing to you. It's not the same between you and me anymore. You used to have a driving passion for our relationship. Now it feels like you've put us on autopilot. And that hurts. So much of the time now, when I talk to you, it feels like you're a million miles away. I am realizing more and more that when you're with me physically, you're somewhere else emotionally. It's so hard to be with you and alone at the same time. When you do engage with me, I don't know whether to duck or pucker. You have been so all over the page lately, I don't know what to do. You used to be able to roll with life's little problems and setbacks. These days it seems like the littlest of things can set you off. That's not the person I used to know. And, while I'm getting less and less of the real you, it seems like you are counting on me more and more to take care of the daily challenges of life. I'm not saying you're dropping the ball at work—I know that's one of your worst fears. But I feel like I'm having to keep all the other plates in life spinning. Now I'm getting worn out.

Vacation last month was really a turning point—that's when I knew we had to do something about this. Given how stressed you'd been, I had so looked forward to getting away and unwinding. I thought I might get the real you back for a full week. You had no idea how exciting that prospect was. And then we got there, and I realized that the real you was back at work. It was like your phone and your laptop were leashes that kept you chained to the stress of your job, and you couldn't come out and play with us, even though it was supposed to be play time. I'm not complaining here about the fact that your work has stolen you from me. We are so past that point. Now I think that your stress has become such a crushing load that no one gets the real you anymore. Not your coworkers, not your friends, not our kids, not even you . . . no one gets the best of you. Work has gotten the best of you, and now you're a shell of who you used to be.

But in my heart, I believe I haven't really lost you yet. The real you is still in there somewhere. And I desperately want to connect with the real you. It's been a long time, and I'd like to get reacquainted. But that won't happen unless you are willing to open your eyes and see that you're not superhuman. You can't fight all the world's battles, and you aren't a failure if you have to let go of a weight that's too heavy to carry. I need the real you . . . the real us. What do you say?

The letter you just read was an amalgamation of things people have said to their burned-out spouses in my office over the years. For thirteen years, I counseled people in distressed marriages. I was often deeply moved by the things the burned-out person's spouse would say. So often they would say things like "I don't know how to help you." They would paint a picture of a crushing stress load that had increasingly sucked the life out of their spouse.

They would talk about their spouse as though they had lost them. Even though their burned-out spouse was very clearly in the room, they would plead for them to come back. They would explain to me that while their spouse was in my office physically, they had checked out mentally. They would tell me that when they did get anything from their spouse, it was wrapped in emotional reactivity. The worse the burnout was, the more desperation I'd hear in the spouse's voice. It was almost like they were asking me to work some magic that would bring their spouse back from the stress abyss. I couldn't do that, of course, but my heart was always deeply moved by what they said.

One wife of a burned-out engineer said it perfectly: "We both know something is terribly wrong. I'm the only one with energy to fight this thing, and he's the only one who knows what's wrong. At least I hope he knows. If not, we're in real trouble."

Earlier in this book I talked about my dad's struggle with burnout that was so profound he had a sort of nervous breakdown. In preparation for the writing of this manuscript, I read my mom's journals from those very dark days. I had her permission to include portions of them in this book, but I opted not to. They are so raw and personal that I felt they should remain private. But as I read through those journals again today, I was impressed with how sad and concerning it is to love someone who is stressed to the breaking point. I'm aware that you may be reading this book not for yourself but for the sake of a loved one who is battling burnout. My heart goes out to you. And I hope to provide some answers and some hope.

Burnout and Emotional Intelligence

These days the self-help shelves of bookstores are stocked with resources on emotional intelligence. There's a reason for that. The more emotionally intelligent you are, the more relational you can be. Emotionally intelligent people know what to do with emotions. They know how to be aware of and process their own emotions, and they know how to perceive and respond to the emotions of others. When your teenager does or says something that aggravates the ever-living crud out of you, but you take a few minutes to think about it and then respond in a way that you're proud of later— that's emotional intelligence. When your coworker is not acting like themselves, and you treat them with grace and understanding, realizing they must be going through something difficult—that's emotional intelligence. And when you're cranky, and you realize it, and you choose to change your thoughts and conclusions so that you change your mood to a positive one—that's emotional intelligence.

The problem is that when you're emotionally exhausted (and remember that we said being exhausted of emotional energy is what burnout is all about), your emotional intelligence takes a major hit. Emotional intelligence is powered by emotional energy. If you have a lot of emotional energy, you have the capacity to be very emotionally intelligent. The less emotional energy you have, the less emotionally intelligent you will be, even if you are normally a very relational person.

So what happens when you run out of emotional energy? First, you will become more emotionally reactive. Things that once would not have bothered you will drive you nuts. You'll go to the mats to fight for small wins in situations where you would once have just rolled with the punches. And you'll find yourself on a wild emotional ride the rest of the time, clinging to an emotional pendulum that swings violently from side to side. As you try to course correct from one emotion that is a little out of balance, you'll feel yourself toggle to a different out-of-balance emotion. And the people around you will feel like they're on a roller-coaster ride that they didn't sign up for.

The problem is that one of the parts of your brain that is most intelligent at helping you process your emotional experience is not functioning very well, compared to how it functioned before you became burned out[1] (we'll talk a lot more about that in the chapter on getting your life back occupationally). Perhaps it's best to put it this way: when you're exhausted, the engine of your emotions is revved up, but your emotional steering wheel and brakes are not very reliable. So you may find yourself unusually chipper at one moment and then unusually morose later on. You may find yourself unusually critical of one person, only to turn around and praise someone else who doesn't really deserve it. To people around you, the unpredictability of your emotions will be unmistakable. They'll know something is wrong.

Emotional exhaustion will also make you less aware of other people's emotions and experiences. It may cause you to come across as unfeeling or completely out of touch when that's not your true self. Of course you care deeply about people and want them to know that their experience matters to you. But if you're emotionally exhausted, chances are you won't be sending that message. Instead, you'll tend to steamroll people without meaning to. And you'll start to notice that people who used to be your allies will start to act as though they'd be happy to vote you off the island.

With those closest to you, emotional exhaustion will look like an extreme imbalance. Because you are dry of emotional energy, you will need others to do the work of processing your emotions for you, and you won't be able to help others with their emotional battles. Your spouse, kids, and closest friends may begin to feel as though your relationship with them is very one-sided.

Because relationships are fueled by emotional intelligence, when you're out of emotional energy, the ones who love you most will likely feel that they must carry all the weight of your relationship. Temporarily, that's not a deal-breaker. And if you're going through a profound episode of burnout, there may be a season when others need to surround you and lift you up with their energy while you do the hard work of replenishing your own emotional resources. That's what happened in my dad's case. But it can't be a long-term strategy. At some point the emotional gas tank has to get refilled if you want your relationships to be healthy.

What Depersonalization Looks Like

For some people, the emotional struggles we just talked about are not enough of a warning sign to inspire change. After going through a season of dealing with no emotional gas in the tank, they hit a place called *depersonalization*.[2] You may remember we talked about depersonalization in chapter 2. It's a stage of burnout in which you start to withdraw from who you really are because you are exhausted of emotional energy. When you experience the shock of realizing you don't have the energy to be yourself anymore, you are confronted with the reality that surviving means backing away from being yourself. So you withdraw from people and activities that you would normally engage with, and you begin to *check out*.

Checking out can happen in a lot of different ways. It can show up as a lack of interest in doing things you used to like to do with other people. It can show up as a sort of quiet, disconnected, flat presence when you're with people. You might not get involved in conversations that you would once have enjoyed, and when people do say something to you or ask you something, they might have to repeat themselves because you weren't really paying attention when they were talking anyway. It can show up as noncommitment in your responses about how you feel about something. A coworker asking you where you would like to have lunch can cause you to be surprisingly unsure of how you should answer. You poll your feelings about something as simple as whether you would like a hamburger or a sub sandwich and, surprisingly, get no internal response. In those moments, what would have previously seemed like the simplest of questions seems strangely complex.

Meanwhile, you may find yourself retreating inwardly to somewhere in your own head. Others wouldn't know it because, again, you seem checked out. But you know that, inside, you're overthinking everything. Even as checked out as you are, you're still feeling the sharp edge of anxiety.

What are people thinking about me? How will I accomplish all the things I need to do? What if I fail? Why is that guy looking at me like that?

Chances are, in that private place where you are trying to process everything from a mental distance, you feel sad and demotivated. You struggle with the feeling that life is moving too fast. If things would just slow down a bit, perhaps you could make better sense of it all.

And, while you're trying to process all of this, your friends and family keep trying to tell you they are noticing something is wrong. Maybe they try to tell you you've taken on too much. Maybe they complain because they feel you're disconnected and distant. Maybe at work you're hearing from coworkers that you need to get your head in the game or that you need to be more present. Regardless, there is a voice inside you that says *I wish they knew how hard I'm fighting just to keep my head above water.*

Earlier I shared about being a marriage counselor and listening to the spouses of burned-out individuals who desperately wanted their spouse back. It took me a long time to realize just how badly burned-out spouses *wanted* to be back. They weren't disconnected because that's how they preferred to be. They were stuck on the side of the road with an empty emotional gas tank, feeling sad because they didn't have the energy they needed to be the best version of themselves. The good news is that I learned that there are solutions that can help a burned-out person get back to the best version of themselves and that can bring that person back to those they love.

All of the Above

At this point in the book, we've already talked about several things you can do to fight the emotional battle of burnout. We've talked about things you can do to bolster your physical and emotional health, and all those things apply here. In this section we'll talk about specific strategies you can use to be more relationally present and emotionally engaged in your relationships, but these strategies will work best if they are part of a holistic approach to burnout that you develop as you read through the entire book. So the first thing you can do to get your life back relationally is *all of the above*, and by that, I mean incorporate what we've covered in previous chapters. Then move on to the three strategies presented here: checking in, doing a mental double take, and leaving the life preserver for the ship.

Checking In

Hopefully by the time you read this section, you'll have a pretty good personal working hypothesis about why we check out when we're burned out. When you don't feel like you have any emotional energy to spare, you'll tend to conserve, conserve, conserve. And one way of conserving emotional energy is to avoid being present with other people unless you absolutely have to. But here I need to make the case that even though you might think you're conserving energy by checking out (and I do think that is our natural go-to way of thinking), you may be making the emotional energy problem worse. When people start checking out, they start experiencing relationship problems. No one wants to be in a relationship with someone who's not present. In the moment it might seem like we're conserving emotional energy by mentally exiting conversations and activities, but when the relational bill comes due, it will be a big one. In the end it costs you more to be emotionally absent than it does to be emotionally present.

So at the risk of sounding as though I'm oversimplifying the facts, I would suggest to you that the easiest way to combat the habit of checking out is to check in. Checking out is something that happens because we hand over the controls of our mental cockpit to autopilot. Checking in, on the other hand, is what we do when we realize we've handed over the controls, and we reverse that decision by piloting our mental plane manually again. It means shelving what you were thinking about when you went somewhere else mentally and putting the activity or conversation in front of you back on the front burner. You may have to humbly ask someone to repeat something to get you back up to speed. That's better than missing the whole interaction.

You can check in by intentionally paying attention to whatever is happening right in front of you. Be observant. What is the room like around you? What color are the eyes of the person speaking to you? If you're at a restaurant and you're eating, how does the food taste? Get centered in the *here and now*. The *there and later* will still be waiting for you to process when this interaction is done. For now, check in. Be present. Not only will you find that, in the long run, it's far less emotionally costly to be present, but you'll also find that you can build emotional energy by engaging with the people and activities around you.

As an academic, I've written some on the topic of mindfulness.[3] It's a hot topic in the world of psychology. And while there is still much for us to learn about mindfulness, this is clear from the research: it can be a tremendously healthy practice mentally and physically. At the heart of mindfulness practice is the choice to check in and not put your brain on autopilot. The opposite of the word *mindfulness* is the word *mindlessness*. And when we talk about checking out, that's what we're talking about. We're talking about the fact that it is possible to go through the motions of life mindlessly—it's just not wise to do so. Mindfulness, at its core, is a decision to not miss out on the here and now, to exercise our own mental power to be observant and engaged, and to limit distractions and temptations to mentally check out.

Let's talk about two important ways you can practice checking in: spending time on those you love and listening authentically.

Spending Time on Those You Love

I'm at that stage of life where our oldest child is getting ready to fly from the nest. She just graduated from high school and is getting ready to attend college out of state. I guess when that happens, it's always cause for a little introspection. What kind of father have I been? Have I been there for her in the way she needed me to be? What will my legacy be as her parent? Perhaps the hardest question for me to address is *Did I spend enough time on her?*

Wait, Jonathan, don't you mean *Did I spend enough time with her?*

Nope. I mean did I spend enough time *on* her.

Time is like money. It's a finite resource, it's valuable, it can be spent, and once it's gone, it's gone. I've come to believe there is a difference between spending time with someone and spending time *on* someone. When I go out to dinner with my wife, I spend money *with* her. If, on the other hand, I go to the local jewelry shop and purchase a bracelet I know my wife has had her eye on, and I give it to her, I spent money *on* her. The truth is that I've spent a lot of time with my two daughters. We've been in each other's presence and spent time together. And I don't want to discount the value of that. It's important to spend time with your loved ones. But I do think, in the grand analysis of my life, it will be likely that I did not spend enough time *on* my two daughters.

Time with someone is not the same as time *for* someone. If you really want to check in with your loved ones in this season of burnout, try being intentional about carving out time *for* your loved ones. Spend some time *on* them. What do they like to do? What are they interested in? What do they love to do with you? In what environment do they tend to open up and share what's on their minds?

Take out a calendar and slot in some spots dedicated to spending time on the people you love. If you're married, start with your spouse. Then, if you have kids, pencil them in. Strike that—pen them in. Think about the friends who care most about you, the people who've been there for you through the ups and downs, then take a moment and light up your calendar with some spots of intentional time spending. You'd be surprised how much easier it is to check in when spending the time on someone was your idea and you're invested in making it happen. Even if it doesn't feel like you have the energy to do this, give it a try, perhaps with one person. My hunch is you'll find that this kind of intentional time spending will start to help refuel your emotional gas tank. It's a win-win.

Listening Authentically

It's strangely difficult to really listen to another person. It takes therapists quite a while to learn the skill. It's not that we're incapable of listening well; most of us are good at listening to people talk about things we find interesting. But, if we're honest, we'd have to admit that we're not great at listening when we get bored or distracted. In those moments, it's easy to check out. We don't announce it to the world. We just quietly, imperceptibly leave the conversation in our heads and go somewhere else. The problem is that inauthentic listening is always a gamble. It's like falling asleep in algebra class. Perhaps you might not need to know what was said for the exam, but you might be surprised.

The truth is that people around us are freakishly good at figuring out when we are actually listening to them and when we are not. And they don't much appreciate it when we don't test well . . . when it's clear that information they gave us never actually attached itself to our little gray cells. All of us are guilty of this. But when you're burned out, you'll be the chief offender. Burnout will cause you to leave conversations even when they are really important and you need to remember what is being said.

Authentic listening, then, is one of the ways you wrestle away the controls from autopilot and take control of your mental presence. How do you listen authentically? Start by mentally setting aside what your go-to mental distraction is. If it's work, if it's some kind of personal worry, if it's a mental problem you can't seem to solve, whatever—set it aside. If doing little mental exercises helps, imagine that you take that mental distraction and lock it away for a bit in a closet. You can always return to the closet later and engage with that issue. But for now, leave it in the closet. If, during your interaction with another person, you find your attention drifting back to that distraction, don't get mad at yourself. Just exercise what I call the huh! reflex. *Huh! I was just distracted by that thing again. It's okay. I'll worry about that later. Back to this conversation . . .*

Second, listen for meaning. Unless someone is learning English as a second language and practicing their vocabulary, they probably aren't talking to you for linguistic practice. They're talking to you in order to *exchange meaning*. They want you to know about their experience and what they're feeling. So instead of viewing the conversation as a content exchange, think of it as a chance to really get into the other person's world by truly receiving the meaning they want to share with you.

Make humble guesses in your mind about what they are trying to convey. *What are they trying to tell me? What is the point they want me to get? What do they want me to know?* By asking these sorts of questions, you will give yourself strong goals in the conversation, and you'll reduce the chances of being bored and disconnected. Conversations have power if you tap into the potential for meaning.

If you want to test whether you're doing a good job at authentic listening, try making a simple reflection of what you think you're understanding from what the other person is saying. It won't take you long to get feedback from the other person that will give you a pretty good idea about how well you're listening. It's not that they will necessarily agree with your reflection. Perhaps you will have missed their point or misjudged what they are trying to say. But if you are in the ballpark, you'll notice that they'll light up a little bit with the understanding that you are tracking with what they are trying to say. If you're a little off, they'll correct you. The fact that you're trying to get what they are saying will still light up their emotional circuits.

Doing a Mental Double Take

Earlier I talked about how emotional reactivity can be one of the biggest problems that comes along with burnout. That emotional reactivity partially happens because the part of our brain that helps process our emotions in the most intelligent way isn't performing at its peak capacity. But the other part of the problem is that, when we check out and put our brain on autopilot, we allow our brain to make automatic decisions about how to interpret what we see and experience. One thing we know is that the brain doesn't like to have to figure the same thing out multiple times.[4] Once it figures something out, it stores what it learned and tries to apply it the next time it needs to process the same thing.

Usually that's very helpful. We need these mental templates to help us make sense of the world around us or we'd never get anything accomplished. For instance, as I write these words, I'm sitting in a study room at the local state university. When I arrived at the study room, I was presented with several things I hadn't seen before. I hadn't seen the exact door to this room before. Yet I didn't have any trouble knowing what it was, what function it performs, and how to use it. There was a table and chairs in the room that I hadn't seen before, but I didn't spend an hour trying to figure out the furniture. I set my laptop on the desk, sat my posterior in the chair, and got right to the business of writer's block.

Similarly, I didn't have any trouble figuring out the chalkboard, the light switch, or the power outlets in the study room. Why? Because the brain is great at fuzzy matching, a term from computer contexts that is also used in neuropsychological circles. It was able to fit this new door into my understanding of *door*. It fit the new study table into my previous understanding of *table*. The brain is brilliant at matching.

All of that matching happened on autopilot. I didn't oversee that process, and it cost me no mental energy to speak of. In fact, it happened below my level of awareness. The way the brain matches things works kind of like this: that looks very much like a table, so it must be a table. That looks very much like a chair, so it must be a chair. That fuzzy matching is great when it comes to evaluating the furniture in a room. It doesn't work so well when it comes to evaluating other people's emotions, intentions, words, or actions. Unfortunately, from a relational standpoint, if you're flying on autopilot, your brain will be happy to *assume* what things mean when you encounter them.

If we have our brain set on autopilot, we may be tempted to see someone's facial expression and assume something about that expression that simply isn't true. Or our brains might fuzzy match what someone said to what someone else said, and we might think that the intent of those two people was the same. Relationships are just too complicated to manage on autopilot. If you let your autopilot interpret what other people mean by what they say, how they act, and what they do, you'll start making a lot of mistakes. And those mistakes lead to that emotional reactivity we were talking about before.

How do you exit autopilot in relationships? Here's a metaphor that I think might help. My wife and I like to do escape rooms. Don't ask me why. We pay someone to lock us up in a room for an hour, and we solve puzzles to get out. For some reason we like solving that sort of puzzle. We've done escape rooms all over the country.

Recently we did an escape room where the initial puzzles were in a living room scene. In the living room was a side table that was supporting a small lamp. Right away I was tempted to assume that lamp was like every other lamp I've ever seen. My thought was that it probably wasn't relevant to the puzzle solving, as lamps only exist to provide light. But when you're in an escape room, you tend to learn to override initial conclusions. I went over and lifted the lamp up and looked for secret compartments. I looked inside the shade to see if any hidden messages were scrawled inside. I turned the lamp on and off to see if it would toggle some sort of escape room gag. Alas, it was just a lamp.

But what I did with that lamp is what we have to do with our initial relational conclusions. When your spouse looks at you with a certain facial expression and your initial interpretation is that they are showing you contempt, you may need to go over and take a closer look at what you're seeing and make sure your initial conclusion was correct. Perhaps it was, but more often than not you'll find there's a hidden compartment in that relational experience. And when you do that sort of mental double take, you'll be surprised how many relational land mines you can sidestep.

Leaving the Life Preserver for the Ship

I can't wrap up a chapter on how to get your life back relationally without talking about how to deal with isolation. Burned-out people isolate. That's just how it is. One of the big reasons for that isolation is the emotional emptiness we've talked about earlier. But one of the other reasons for isolation is that in order to stay connected with others, you have to be able to trust others. The more burned out you are, the less you will be able to trust others. And as trust goes down in your life, control will go up. Another way of putting it is that you will grasp for control of every area of your life where you are struggling to trust others.

Imagine you are on a cruise ship and you become convinced that you cannot trust the captain, the ship mechanics, or your fellow passengers. So you demand a situation in which you are in complete control of your own well-being. Such a situation can be arranged, but it's not necessarily a good thing. Let's say, then, that you find yourself afloat outside the ship with a life preserver. Now you are in complete control; you have what you asked for. But you've ended up in a much more dangerous situation than the one you were in before.

The truth is we are in the most danger when we decide we can trust only ourselves. I'm not making the case that everyone is trustworthy. And I'm not making the case that if you trust people you'll never be let down. The case I am making is that we weren't meant to do life alone, and existence with just the life preserver is lonely and scary.

One of the most important things you can do to get your life back relationally is to make some wise decisions about whom to trust in your life and to get on the ship with them. Let them speak into your life and your situation. You've already done that to some extent with me by picking up this book. And, while I'm proud to welcome you back to the ship, you'll need some people close to you who can really help you sail through the waters of life. Think about who your close circle should be, then decide that you will let them have a seat at the table. You'll thank yourself later.

A Biblical Perspective

One place where you can really see the relational costs of burnout in Scripture is in the later part of Luke 10. Jesus is visiting the town of Bethany, where he had three close friends: Mary, Martha, and Lazarus. In this passage, Jesus's friends were to host a special dinner for him and his entourage. It was dinner for fifteen . . . at least.

Imagine, for a moment, trying to prepare a special dinner for over a dozen guests, one of whom is the Savior of the world. That's stressful enough. But add to that the stress of not having a grocery store from which to buy the food. Imagine trying to clean the house without a vacuum. Imagine preparing the food without the aid of a refrigerator, a microwave, or a modern oven. If you get yourself grounded in what the stress of that must have been like, you are beginning to understand what it may have been like for Martha.

She was beside herself trying to pull off an amazing dinner for her beloved guests. Like anyone who has tried to host a large event, she was probably dealing with all sorts of details that were going sideways, and she was likely exhausted from putting out fires and trying to make this dinner happen. Imagine her consternation when she realized she was getting no help from her sister, Mary. When she looked for her absent sister, she found her sitting at Jesus's feet, listening to him teach rather than helping with the meal.

In verse 40 of Luke 10, we see Martha have a little bit of an emotional breakdown. She stomps into that living room and vents to Jesus. She tries to get Jesus to see how wrong it is that Mary is not helping her, and then she orders Jesus to tell Mary to get in that kitchen and help her. My hunch is that things got really quiet in that room when Martha came in and let Jesus have it with both barrels. But Jesus's response is important for anyone who is dealing with the emotional fallout of burnout. Here's what he said:

> But the Lord said to her, "My dear Martha, you are worried and upset over all these details! There is only one thing worth being concerned about. Mary has discovered it, and it will not be taken away from her."

Luke 10:41-42

There you have it. Jesus diagnosed the relational challenges of burnout—worry and distraction. The original word in the Greek that is translated "worried" here carries with it the idea of being pulled in different directions[5] to the point that our entire self is in a state of disruption. It is as close to the biblical definition of depersonalization as we are likely to see in Scripture.

And the word translated as "upset" comes from a Greek word that means to be mentally bothered—to have a "riot" going on inside.[6] What is it like emotionally to be burned out? It's like waking up one day and realizing that you are being pulled in so many different directions that you don't remember what it is like to be at peace. It's like walking around with that cloud overhead that doesn't seem to dissipate. That hazy fog of disturbance won't leave you alone and let you be.

Martha had depersonalized. She wasn't the best version of herself, and her emotional reactivity had brought her to a place where she was ordering Jesus Christ around. Grasping a life preserver of control, she was barking orders back up to the ship, demanding that those she could no longer trust do things her way. Jesus graciously calmed her down and reminded her of the power of being present. Mary was doing that—she realized the power in that moment of being tethered to the relationally important thing that was going on: Jesus was teaching. Mary was spending time on Jesus, she was listening authentically, and she was being energized emotionally by her relationship with Jesus.

You can get your life back relationally. Follow Mary's example, and you'll be surprised how quickly you see your relationships improve and that R score on your PERSON chart start to climb.

CHAPTER 5
Group Discussion Questions

1. Have you ever noticed that you were on relationship auto-pilot? What did you do about it?

2. What barriers do you face when it comes to being present in relationships with those you love?

3. How do you know if someone is listening to you authentically? How can you listen authentically to those you love?

4. What has your experience been in trying to spend time on those you love? When was a time that you specifically remember being intentional to devote special time to and focus on someone special in your life? How did that impact the relationship?

5. What would you consider to be the biblical take on the value of relationships versus the power of achievements?

Getting Your Life Back Spiritually

On December 21, 2010, I drove to my parents' house to spend some time with my dad, who was going through the nervous breakdown I described in chapter 4. While I had been told he was improving, I was shocked when I saw him. The warm smile he always greeted me with was gone. Instead of jumping up out of his chair and greeting me with a hug, as he normally would have done, he remained seated in a sort of hunched-forward position. We didn't make eye contact because he was staring off into space. Because my parents were going to be traveling again to get him help over the next several days, they would be gone over Christmas. My younger brother who still lived at home was opening his Christmas gift, which they had just given him in anticipation of being gone. The irony was painful for all of us. It didn't feel like Christmas. It didn't feel like the time to exchange gifts. It felt like the world was falling apart.

I desperately wanted to understand what my dad was going through. He tried to explain it to me. There was a physical component to what he was going through. He was sure he was dying, and he did have some worrisome symptoms. In retrospect, I think those symptoms were caused by the stress he was experiencing. At the time, he was convinced that he had cancer. There was clearly an emotional component. As I described in chapter 3, he toggled back and forth between anxiety and depression, and I remember being shocked by it. I had never really seen my dad weep before. It was like I was sitting across from a completely different person. But there was also a component of what he told me that shocked me more than any of the rest of what he had to say. *There was a spiritual component to this.*

"I don't think God has ever really used me; whatever ministry success I've had must have been in the arm of the flesh," he told me repeatedly. It made no sense. Of course God had used him. In fact, the success of NewSpring Church had been so meteoric and conspicuous that pastors from around the country were consistently contacting us, hoping to get insight on how to have similar success in their ministries. With dad out of pocket, I had been fielding a lot of these calls, and it had made me even more aware of how uncommon the sort of growth we'd experienced was.

It wasn't in the "arm of the flesh." That's kind of an old-school way of saying that success is generated from human hype and not from the power of God. But that wasn't how it was. In fact, when people called to find out how to replicate our success other places, our answer was that we weren't responsible for the success—God was. We would tell them there was no magic formula and no prescribed set of steps. God was blessing us, and our primary goal was to stay in his will and out of his way. That attitude of humility was something my dad instilled in all of us by modeling it. He wasn't about platform building, and he was not a credit taker. His primary interest was in following God closely so that we could reach our full destiny as a church.

But to hear my dad talk at this point, you'd think he had spent his ministry career disconnected from God, going through the motions. *How could he think that?* I wondered. Someone who might not know him as well as I do might think he was confessing a deep, dark secret of being a spiritual fake. I knew better. At the time, I hypothesized that whatever was attacking him physically and emotionally must also be attacking him spiritually. Now I'm sure that was the case.

Over the past thirteen years in my counseling work, I've learned that burnout can leave you feeling like a fraud spiritually. It can leave you feeling as though your faith isn't real, that you're a complete failure, and that you have no real connection with God. At a time when you need God more than ever, dealing with burnout can leave you feeling as though you have no capacity to connect with God.

In our conversation, my dad looked at me and said, "How do you know for sure you're saved?" I didn't know how to respond. Was this an impromptu theological quiz? If so, it seemed remarkably ill-timed. Was my dad asking because he was worried about my spiritual condition? After all, he was convinced he was dying. Perhaps he wanted reassurance about my spiritual condition should anything happen to him. After a little more conversation, I realized he was looking for reassurance about *his* spiritual condition. Looking back, I remember I didn't give an answer to his question. I was too busy having an out-of-body experience. As a twenty-nine-year-old trying to find my footing in this new world of full-time pastoral ministry, I couldn't believe I was sitting across from my dad, my pastor, my boss . . . and he might not be sure he was saved.

I thought back to my growing-up years. I'd never heard anyone explain the gospel message as clearly as my dad. I felt certain that he understood and embraced the gospel. I'd watched him model the life of a sincere follower of God. I'd never heard my dad say a foul word . . . ever.[1] I'd watched as he had lived above reproach in his dealing with members of the opposite sex, in his avoidance of addictive substances, and in his daily decision-making. He was the real deal. I can truly say that my dad was at home who he was at church. There weren't two versions of my dad. He was an example of the kind of Christian I wanted to be. Could a person fake that sort of thing and still not be saved? I suppose so. But I didn't think it was very likely in my dad's case.

It was apparent to me at that moment that there were two realities present in that room. There was the true reality of my dad's spiritual condition, and there was whatever reality my dad was seeing at the time, which was clearly inaccurate, distorted, and alarming.

If you are a God follower and you're dealing with burnout, you may be dealing with that same sort of distorted view of reality. Burnout will impact you spiritually. It may not exhibit itself the same way it did with my dad, but burnout can deliver some powerful punches that bruise the soul.

Refining Fire

Several days later, my parents were traveling to get my dad counseling. At the hotel where they were staying, my dad pulled his laptop out and began to write. He wrote about how a person can know they are saved. The language wasn't flowery, and the concepts weren't abstract. It was simple, straightforward, and authentic—the written notes from a believer's journey to remind himself of the truths that touch eternity. As he typed those words, he was processing for himself, at the most basic level possible, what he knew to be true about God's nature. As a debater from way back, he made a case—to himself and anyone else who would read what he was writing later on—for how a person could know they were a member of God's family and that they were going to heaven.

Not only did that exploration of his faith—the refining fire of a faith crisis—bring him back into reassurance of his own spiritual standing with God, it also became the manuscript for a short book that has since been given out to tens of thousands of people right after they've accepted Christ. I heard my dad present the gospel hundreds of times before his 2010 breakdown. And I've heard him present the gospel hundreds of times since. I can't prove it, but I think there is greater power in the way he presents it now. I think there is a deeper compassion there for those struggling to know where they stand with God. There is a more personal appeal from a heart that remembers how painful it was to feel spiritually disconnected.

My point is this: if you're going through a season of spiritual pain because of your battle with burnout, it may help to know that you are on the cusp of a connection with God that is deeper and more meaningful than what you have experienced up until now. While it would be really easy for you right now to get wrapped up in scripts of shame and spiritual doubt, let me encourage you not to go there. Instead, I want to encourage you to do what my dad did . . . to revisit what you can know for sure about where you stand with God. In this chapter, I'll share some important concepts to remember as you battle burnout.

Remember that when you're exhausted, it's not a time to move away from God, it's a time to move toward him. Jesus said this:

> Then Jesus said, "Come to me, all of you who are weary and carry heavy burdens, and I will give you rest. Take my yoke upon you. Let me teach you, because I am humble and gentle at heart, and you will find rest for your souls. For my yoke is easy to bear, and the burden I give you is light."
>
> Matthew 11:28–30

Check out the first three words of what Jesus says to an exhausted person: "Come to me." He is ready to help you win this battle with burnout. I want to share with you some key things to remember that will help you experience the soul rest that Jesus promised.

God Loves You, and He Cares

In John 4, Jesus encounters a person who is often called either the "Samaritan woman" or "the woman at the well." Jesus met this woman as he traveled through Samaria on his way to Galilee. Arriving at the well in Sychar at roughly the same time as this woman, Jesus asked her for a drink. That was weird.

First of all, self-respecting Jewish teachers didn't tend to show their faces in Samaria, as there were some really hard feelings between Samaritans and Jews. Beyond this, in the male-dominated culture of the day, it was unusual for a man of any standing to speak directly to a woman in public to whom he wasn't related— especially to ask for a favor.[2] The other thing that was weird about the encounter was that this woman was there at that time of day.

Bible scholars point out that women would not normally come to draw water from the well at noontime, which was the hottest part of the day.[3] Drawing water was an early morning or late evening activity. The temperature was much more favorable that way. A long walk and the physical exertion of carrying water a long distance in the hot noontime sun was not ideal. Yet this lady came at noon. Why?

Chances are this lady showed up at noon because she didn't really want to engage with anyone. She had enough stress in her life without having to deal with the sideways glances and whispers of the community gossip chain. She knew what they were saying about her. She was the woman in town who couldn't keep a man. She'd been married five times. Five times it ended badly and she had to start over. Now she was living with a guy who was willing to be her sex partner but not her husband.

Every day was stressful. Every day was a day with regrets about the past. And, as far as the future was concerned . . . how reliable could it be with a guy who wasn't willing to put a ring on her finger? At this point, life was about survival. She just needed to make it from one day to the next. Emotionally, though, the wounds ran deep. And the longer she lived with the wounds, the more tired she became. It was too much for a person to carry.

Frankly, I think that's why Jesus decided to go through Samaria on the way to Galilee. I think he knew there was a woman in Sychar who was on the bleeding edge of a full-on burnout breakdown, and he wanted her to know that God loved her and cared about her situation. Knowing how exhausted she was from having to come get water every day in the midday heat, Jesus used water as a metaphor to tell her about what he wanted to do for her. He told her that if she asked him, he could give her a new spring of water that would bubble up inside her and that she would never be thirsty again. She didn't realize it was a metaphor at first, but eventually, Jesus would help her understand that he was offering her eternal life and a chance to start over. Interestingly, the refining fire of her faith crisis caused her to be one of the first documented missionaries of all time, as she went back to the community she had once avoided to convince them to come and meet Jesus, too.

The metaphor of the water might be a bit hard to grasp in our modern world, but think about the metaphor I've been using throughout this book—a gas tank. Suppose you went to fill up your car at the gas station and met Jesus there. And suppose he told you that if you were to ask him, he could give you a supply of fuel that would never run out. I'd be on board! But like the water metaphor in John 4, Jesus isn't talking about something as trivial as household water or gasoline for your car. Jesus is offering spiritual energy—the power (as Scripture says) to become the children of God. Jesus is offering a relationship in which we cannot be separated from his love by the stressors we experience in this world (Romans 8:38–39). He is offering his light burden in exchange for our heavy one (Matthew 11:28–30).

For some of us, we've accepted that gift a long time ago, but we have let our relationship with God fall so far to the bottom of our priorities list that the spiritual energy God wants to give us is blocked by the worries and distractions of this world or the desire for things and achievements (Mark 4:19). But the spiritual energy God gives us comes in the form of this gift—God loves you. God loves you so much that he cares about whatever is draining you of energy. He cares about what you're going through at work. He cares about what is happening in your family situation. He cares about your financial burdens. He cares about your search for meaning and purpose in life.

So let me encourage you to stop for a moment today and ask yourself if you have allowed God an opportunity to infuse your life with the spiritual energy he is offering. Or is the highway to your heart jammed with the traffic of things that don't really matter? Perhaps this burnout crisis is an opportunity to refine your connection to God. Perhaps it's an opportunity to sweep out the spiritual cobwebs and start fresh with a passion for God that you lost somewhere along the way.

God Will Help You with Life's Stresses If You'll Let Him

In Exodus 14, the Israelites were in the process of escaping from Egypt, where they had been terribly mistreated as slaves. Following God's directions, the Israelites ended up at the banks of the Red Sea with no clear path forward. The Pharaoh, realizing that the Israelites weren't just leaving for a few days (as they had originally suggested) and that they were instead escaping permanently, went after them. I can't imagine what sort of stress the Israelites must have felt when they realized they couldn't move forward (because of the Red Sea) and they couldn't escape backward because the Egyptians were chasing them down. The Bible tells us that the people panicked. That's fair. I would have panicked, too. But Moses, giving instructions on behalf of God, said this: "Don't be afraid. Just stand still and watch the LORD rescue you today. The Egyptians you see today will never be seen again. The LORD himself will fight for you. Just stay calm" (Exodus 14:13–14).

Stand still and watch, huh? That's not my spiritual gift! I have been officially diagnosed with ADHD, and my hunch is I would also probably be diagnosed with an anxiety disorder were I to be tested for one. I'm a lot better at nervous movement than at standing still. But there are seasons in our spiritual life when we are so outclassed by the problem we're facing that the best thing we can do is stand still and let God do what only he can do.

You likely know the story—God would do the miracle of parting the Red Sea so that the Israelites passed between walls of water on dry ground. That was a solution the Israelites weren't capable of managing, and it wasn't something Moses could do on his own either. Some stresses in life require solutions that are bigger than we are. And when that's the case, we have to develop an ability to stand still and watch God go to work. The good news is that if you're following God as best you know how, God will, as Moses told the Israelites, fight for you. That's why we can stay calm, even when we would typically panic. In our hearts we can be centered on the reality that God is watching over and fighting for us when we go through a tough time. As Jesus reminds us in Matthew 10, God deeply values us and notices our hardships:

> What is the price of two sparrows—one copper coin? But not a single sparrow can fall to the ground without your Father knowing it. And the very hairs on your head are all numbered. So don't be afraid; you are more valuable to God than a whole flock of sparrows.
>
> Matthew 10:29–31

The Fight Against Temptation Will Be Harder Right Now

We all fight battles with temptation. Satan knows if he can get us to mess up in these areas, he can create distance between us and God, and he can amp up our sense of shame and self-frustration. It's very important for you to know that if you are going through a season of burnout, those battles with temptation will be much more difficult. In the next chapter we'll talk about how burnout reduces activity in your brain's prefrontal cortex, and how that reduced activity can wreak havoc at work and in other areas of your life. But for now, it's important to know that the prefrontal cortex of your brain is highly responsible for helping you weigh the future consequences of your current actions.[4] When the pre-frontal cortex is working at its best, you are more likely to say no to temptations with big price tags. When you're burned out, you won't be as likely to make the right call.

Over the years, I've seen dozens of cases of Christian leaders who got mired in some sort of moral failure, and I've wondered if this was part of the reason. In some of these cases, I've known the Christian leader personally, and I can vouch for the fact that their passion for the Lord and their desire to do the right thing seemed very genuine. But we all know that even a person with a very genuine desire to do the right thing can be overcome by temptation to do the wrong thing. That's why it's very important to be aware that in a season of burnout you may be less prepared to fight the temptation battle, and you may need to beef up the safeguards in your life against the temptations that you know you struggle hardest against.

If you find yourself struggling with a specific temptation, let me encourage you to use the example of Joseph from the book of Genesis in the Old Testament as a template for what to do. Joseph was working in the house of Potiphar, his Egyptian master, when Potiphar's wife became sexually attracted to him. She tried to get him to sleep with her time and again. Keep in mind that Joseph is a young man with typical young man hormones, drives, and desires. Potiphar's wife was likely a trophy wife, and the prospect of sex with her probably would have been very desirable. Joseph knew, though, that he shouldn't go there. And he said no.

He made his position very clear:

> But Joseph refused. "Look," he told her, "my master trusts me with everything in his entire household. No one here has more authority than I do. He has held back nothing from me except you, because you are his wife. How could I do such a wicked thing? It would be a great sin against God."
>
> Genesis 39:8–9

Potiphar's wife was not willing to take no for an answer. She kept trying to get Joseph into bed, and so Joseph did all he could to avoid any situation where they would be alone together: "She kept putting pressure on Joseph day after day, but he refused to sleep with her, and *he kept out of her way as much as possible*" (Genesis 39:10, emphasis added).

One day she managed to get him alone, and she grabbed him by his robe as a power play to try to draw him close and get him to give her what she had been asking for: "She came and grabbed him by his cloak, demanding, 'Come on, sleep with me!' Joseph tore himself away, but he left his cloak in her hand as he ran from the house" (Genesis 39:12). She was holding on so tight and he pulled away so hard that she actually ended up holding his robe in her hand. She got his robe, but he kept his integrity.

The rest of the story is fascinating, and I hope you have time to explore the life of Joseph if you haven't already. While turning down Potiphar's wife at this point in Joseph's life started another season of hardship over the next several years of his life, it ultimately positioned him to be the key leader in Egypt for most of the rest of his life. He had shown God that he was trustworthy and able to discipline himself to do the right thing, and God knew he could be promoted to the highest levels of leadership.

So what can we learn from Joseph about how to deal with temptation? The first thing is to *say no*. Just as Joseph went on record with Potiphar's wife that he would not sleep with her, you may need to be on record that you will not do the thing that you are tempted to do. Second, you need to *voluntarily stay away* as much as you can. Just as Joseph stayed away from Potiphar's wife as much as he could, you need to stay away from the sources of temptation in your life. And that means saying no to some things that are not necessarily sinful because you know they could lead to situations where the temptation to sin will be much higher. For instance, you may have to say no to hanging out with certain friends. You may need to tell your coworkers that you aren't going to hit the bar with them after work. You may need to discipline yourself not to get on the computer unless others are present and able to see what you are doing. If you want to fight temptation, you need to stay away as much as you can.

Finally, *run if you have to*. There was a moment when Joseph knew his only two options were to let temptation overtake him or to run for his life. He made the right choice. There will be moments in your life when you know you are too close to temptation, and there will be that small voice in the back of your head that tells you that you could still run away. Listen to that small voice.

Embrace the Struggle; Stiff-Arm the Shame

One of the things that seems to be a reliable struggle for people dealing with burnout is shame and spiritual second-guessing. When people are dealing with burnout they tend to wonder where they stand with God, to question whether they have been some sort of a spiritual fake, and to rake themselves over the spiritual coals. However, that sort of spiritual wallowing rarely leads us closer to God. In fact, it tends to cause us to struggle with deep feelings of unworthiness. Just as our feelings of not being good enough can cause us to withdraw from those we love, from our work, and from our own sense of self, they can cause us to withdraw from God. But the more you count on your relationship with God to be a source of peace and direction in your life, the more painful that withdrawal will be and the more your shame will create a personal crisis.

Wallowing in shame won't get you closer to God. Neither will obsessing about the ways in which you aren't good enough for him. None of us are good enough to earn a relationship with God. We are adopted into his family; we didn't compete to get in. And, as adopted children, we are loved by our father in moments when we succeed, in moments when we fail, and in moments when we are struggling to go on. It does not pay at all to spend sleepless nights trying to figure out how to be worthy of God's love when we are already receiving buckets of that love regardless of our performance.

While refusing to let shame take over, we probably would do well to embrace the spiritual struggle that comes along with burnout. Sometimes in the dark moments of exhaustion, we get a moment of clarity from the Lord—the result of that refining fire I mentioned earlier. For Jacob in the Old Testament, it came in the form of a lesson—that sometimes you have to fight diligently for what you need instead of tricking people to get it—and in the form of a new name: Israel. For Job it came in the form of a renewed realization that God is bigger than our way of thinking about things. For Elijah it came in the form of God's refusal to end his life and a calling to a second season of ministry. For Peter it came in the form of Jesus's invitation back to ministry, even though he thought his denials of Christ were enough of a failure to consign him back to a life of being a fisherman. For Saul (who became the apostle Paul) it came in the form of the realization that he was playing for the wrong team.

A wise (and probably stressed) person once said, "Never let a good crisis go to waste." This burnout crisis in your life can have a refining effect on your character and can propel you into a future that outclasses your past. Don't let shame rob you of that opportunity. Instead, embrace the struggle and the lessons it can bring you. In fact, you might want to keep a journal somewhere in which you list the lessons you're learning as you struggle with burnout. My hunch is that at first you won't know exactly what to write in that journal, but before this thing is over, you may need a second notebook.

Dig a Well

In Psalm 84, we read about the Israelites as they were making their way back to Jerusalem after being in Babylonian captivity for decades. Unlike the sort of group exodus that took place when

Moses led the Israelites from Egypt to the promised land, this journey home for the Israelites would be a scattered one. So the psalmist is writing about people on their way home at all stages of the journey. He's writing about people who have already made it home to Jerusalem when he says "those who dwell in your house" (Psalm 84:4 NIV). And he's talking about those who are on their way but haven't made it there yet when he refers to those "whose strength is in [God], whose hearts are set on pilgrimage" (v. 5 NIV).

Imagine how it must have been for those who hadn't arrived home yet. It's hard when you are going through a rough season and you know that others have made it through and you haven't yet. Specifically, the psalmist talks about one stage of the journey—the passing through the Valley of Baka. That valley was sometimes called the "Valley of Tears"[5] for two reasons. One reason is because of the trees that were found in that arid part of the desert. When the bark on that kind of tree cracks or is split, sap comes out in a way that looks almost exactly like a human tear.[6] When you walk past those trees, it looks like the foliage around you is crying. How depressing. In addition, this valley referenced here, whether metaphorical or literal, would be characterized as a very dry and inhospitable place along the journey.[7]

So think about what it must have been like to walk through that Valley of Tears, knowing that some of your friends and family members were already home in Jerusalem partying joyfully after having made it home. You might think that the psalmist would make the point of how depressing that experience would be. Instead, he makes the point that for those who find their strength in God as they go through this difficult part of the journey, they start digging wells ("make it a place of springs" v. 6 NIV).

Why dig wells? Two reasons. The first is that these individuals anticipate God's provision. There is a spirit in them that says, "It may be dry here, but I bet God has water for us somewhere. I better grab a shovel." There is faith that says, "Even though I'm going through a difficult time, God's provision is here if I look for it."

Second, these well diggers care about those who will make this journey after them. They are interested in being a source of God's provision for people who will follow them through this difficult valley they are in.

So the questions are these: Are you anticipating God's provision as you go through this valley of burnout? If not, you may want to grab a shovel. God's provision is there. You'll just have to look for it. And are you willing to let your burnout journey inspire you to help others who will come through this valley after you do? If so, you may want to start thinking about what digging wells looks like in your context. Maybe God has a whole new season of ministry lined up for you that you will only be able to do because of the valley you're walking through right now.

Don't forget to dig a well.

CHAPTER 6
Group Discussion Questions

1. How has stress impacted your relationship with God?

2. Does it feel like sometimes you have to carry the weight of stress all by yourself? What has been your experience of giving your burdens to God (see Psalm 55:22)? Have you found a practical way to do that?

3. What has been your experience with temptation in the middle of your stress? How have you dealt with temptation that comes up when you're low on energy to fight it?

4. Have you felt shame in your stress journey, especially feeling like you're just not handling your stress as well as you should? What do you think Jesus would say about those feelings?

5. What is your take on how God feels about his children dealing with heavy stress burdens?

Getting Your Life Back Occupationally

Harper nudged her car into the parking space with her name on it in the hospital parking garage. The sign read: "Dr. Walsh, ER Physician." She remembered a time when that sign was a huge source of pride for her. It marked her arrival at a goal she had worked for years to achieve. Becoming an ER doc hadn't been a fast or easy journey, but she'd made it. People looked up to her, and she was making a difference in patients' lives. When she first started working at the hospital, her mother took her picture next to her gleaming reserved parking sign. Now the sign was dirty, like the rest of the parking garage, and it seemed to be more of a tombstone than an achievement marker. It seemed like just another way for the hospital to ensure they had *every second* of her available time. They gave her a parking space near the ER for the same reason big dairies don't let the cows wander off far from the milking stalls.

She sat in her car for three minutes, watching the clock in her car blink the time. In the early days of her medical career, she would have bounced into the ER whenever she happened to get to the hospital, even if it had been fifteen or twenty minutes early. Now she was determined not to go in a minute earlier than she had to. She noticed that in these short periods of time when she was waiting to go in to work, she felt more and more restless. She was really starting to feel a knot in her throat as the time arrived to go in. Part of her didn't want to do this anymore.

But I have to.

Wow. That was a disturbing thought.

She *had* to do this.

Her student debt attested to that fact. She bought some self-help tapes and tried to listen to them just before work. She tried a bit of meditation. She even tried arriving at work at exactly the right time so she wouldn't have to sit there until her shift started. Nothing she tried helped her feel better.

When she entered the ER, her coworkers greeted her, but she noticed they didn't make eye contact. There was a part of her that understood why. Over the last six months, she had become less patient with coworkers. After all, she was a doctor. Doctors are not supposed to suffer fools gladly. And in this profession, if you messed up, people could die. She realized she had been taking everything very seriously, and she had barked at several coworkers. She wasn't ready to apologize for that, though. If they couldn't stand the pressure, perhaps they should leave the ER. Beyond that, perhaps they were just uncomfortable with a woman taking a hard-line stance with a coworker. If so, that was their problem. They needed to get with the times and get a clue.

Her insistence that coworkers not make mistakes was complicated, though, by the fact that Harper had been making mistakes lately. They hadn't been huge mistakes, but she'd noticed she just wasn't on top of her game. She'd definitely had some embarrassing moments when calling a coworker on the carpet for a mistake only to find out that the mistake was hers. Those were moments she'd prefer to forget. She did wonder why she was having those kinds of issues. She'd never been a mistake maker before. Worse, she had been dealing with memory issues. She was asking people to repeat themselves a lot. And, lately, she had started mixing up details of patient symptoms in her head. She would think that Bob in room 5 had a latex allergy when it was really David in room 3. Thank goodness for medical records, charts, and attentive nurses. But it was really concerning that her memory could be that unreliable. It didn't used to be that way.

One thing that had been on her mind a lot lately was that she was going to have to give an account to a medical review board for a death that happened on her watch recently. In the process of trying to revive a coded trauma patient, she had made a decision that others in the room had questioned. While she hadn't told anyone this out loud, she now questioned that decision, too. Now, looking back, she considered it to be a rash, flailing choice that she would not have made if she had managed her emotions and remained calm—as emergency room physicians are required to do.

Toward the end of her shift, Harper took a bathroom break and caught a glimpse of herself in the mirror. Who was this woman she was seeing? And where was the chipper, excited, self-controlled, brilliant female physician she used to be? She had fought so hard to get to this place in her career. But she couldn't imagine anyone wanting to fight to feel the way she did. Deep down, she knew she was burned out. What she didn't know was how she got there or what she could do about it.

Harper's Battle with Burnout Brain

Harper is dealing with something I like to refer to as burnout brain. In short, burnout brain looks like some combination of the following: forgetfulness, agitation, impulsivity, stubbornness, anxiety, depression, restlessness, anger, shortsightedness, and fatigue. When you have burnout brain, work is more difficult, and it can cause you to start feeling negatively about a job you otherwise love. When your brain is suffering from the adverse effects of burnout, everything gets more difficult. It's like running with weights or walking with a ruck pack . . . you feel the downward drag of an extra weight on you that makes everything more difficult.

Like when a person reads the same sentence twenty times because they are being perpetually distracted as they try to read a book, burnout brain will make you feel as though your thoughts have slowed down.[1] Even though you order your brain to focus, it won't.[2] Burnout brain makes you less mindful of everyday tasks. You find yourself going through the motions of everyday routines, on autopilot to such an extent that after you've completed the task, you realize you don't remember even doing it. Little things bother you, and it takes you longer to get over them than it used to. You find yourself keyed up and anxious at some moments and then sad and hollow later on—but you don't know why.

The creative well dries up when you have burnout brain.[3] You demand ideas of yourself, but instead you get anxiety that you won't ever come up with anything new or useful ever again. And despite your desire to think new, creative thoughts, you find yourself stubbornly holding to what has worked before, even if you have a good reason to believe it won't work moving forward.

Listening to others is harder. Like for the children in the Peanuts series of cartoons, the voices of people talking to you sometimes almost seem like distorted background noise. In those moments, you're lost somewhere deep inside yourself. But the journey inward doesn't seem to be helping. Meanwhile, others seem frustrated at how distracted you now seem to be. Compounding these struggles, you'll notice that you're reacting more and filtering less.[4] You'll say things you would never have said years ago. You may do things you later regret. And your relationships will be increasingly tense.

A person with burnout brain will likely exhibit at least some of the following:

- Forgetfulness
- Inflexibility

- Impulsivity
- Emotional outbursts
- Checked-out moments
- Rigidity/lack of creative or innovative thinking
- Perfectionism
- Procrastination
- Anxiety (sometimes accompanied by a nearly childlike dependence on others)
- Depression (especially characterized by an unwillingness or lack of ability to do reasonable life tasks, feelings of hopelessness, and cynicism about self and work)
- Rapid cycling between emotional states
- Self-doubt (this might seem to be the opposite of rigidity, but like emotional states, rigidity and self-doubt tend to cycle back and forth in burned-out individuals)
- Fatalism about self and future

That's what Harper is dealing with. It's not that she's a bad physician or that she's not cut out for this type of work. She's pushed too hard for too long, and she has a major case of burnout brain. In the next section, I'll try to talk a little bit about what happens to our brains when we get burned out. A physician like Harper would probably say I'm oversimplifying things, but this is at least a good start when it comes to understanding the ways our brain buckles under the load of burnout.

Chief Executive Cortex

Right behind your eyebrows, protected by the frontal bone of your skull, is the most advanced part of your brain: the prefrontal cortex. This part of your brain was designed by God to do the heaviest lifting cognitively and emotionally. Emotionally, this part of our brain is deeply involved in the way we process the meaning of things that happen to us, and it is involved in relaying information to and from other parts of the brain and the body about how we feel about our interpretation of those things (our emotional experience). The prefrontal cortex is especially involved with something we call executive functions. Executive functions include things like long-range planning, puzzle/problem-solving, impulse control, temptation resistance, attention/focus control, and cognitive flexibility.[5] Much like the functions of a CEO in a large company, the executive functions of the brain are critical to success, especially if life is throwing major stressors your way.

Unfortunately, we've learned that the prefrontal cortex is one of the parts of the brain that is most vulnerable to the effects of chronic stress,[6] so some of the problematic symptoms of burnout involve reduced executive functions (burnout brain).[7] One of the things we see in burned-out individuals, for instance, is difficulty regulating mood, so it's common for people with burnout to have anxiety, depression, or both. Even if you don't deal with full-on depression or anxiety, that mood-regulation deficit can result in struggles with controlling your emotional responses to everyday life.

You may find yourself weeping for no reason, you may find yourself anxious about things that would never have worried you before, or you might find yourself snapping at others in anger or losing your temper easily. This struggle with emotion regulation is a very common symptom of burnout, and it should not be ignored. Your emotions are sort of a private world, so few will know as well as you when something is off emotionally. When you sense that, it's important to take it seriously.

Stubbornness

Cognitive flexibility takes a hit when our prefrontal cortex is not functioning at its best, so we can become very rigid in our adherence to our own initial thoughts about how something should be done, especially preferring the way we are most comfortable doing something (the "my-way-or-the-highway mentality").

Henry Ford provided a great example of this sort of cognitive rigidity when, after returning from a European vacation, he was presented with a full-size prototype of a new Ford car that had been designed by his team while he was away. Stuck in a protracted season of cognitive rigidity, Ford had been insisting that the Model T did not need a replacement, even though Ford's competitors were turning out new models every year. Ford's staff, I suppose, had hoped that the new car would be attractive and exciting enough to override Ford's insistence on sticking with the old, the familiar, and the comfortable.

After walking around the car and looking at it briefly, Ford proceeded to tear the car apart by hand as his staff looked on.[8] Imagine what it must have been like to see Henry Ford rip the doors off that gleaming new car! That may be an extreme example of cognitive rigidity, but it's a great caricature of what happens when we get burned out and insist on doing things our way.

Impulse Control

Probably one of the biggest challenges of burnout brain has to do with impulse control. Every day we have emotional impulses that may or may not be smart. Some of those impulses may even be below our awareness. For instance, at a very reactive emotional level, we might be tempted to yell at someone who cuts in front of us in the self-checkout line at the grocery store. Or, perhaps more innocently, we might be tempted to binge on an unhealthy food we've been successfully avoiding for the past month when we see it on a store shelf.

The prefrontal cortex has very strong veto power over these sorts of impulses because it makes us more aware of consequences and helps us use long-term rewards as an incentive to say no to short-term temptation.[9] But when we're burned out, we can become far less attuned to the consequences of our choices. It makes sense, then, that when we are burned out, we aren't in a very good position to make big decisions that involve risk. And, in fact, we may need some oversight in making decisions that could have long-term financial, relational, or health ramifications until we are in a better frame of mind.

In Scripture there's a book called Ecclesiastes where Solomon, considered the wisest man in the Bible, journals about his experience with burnout and depression. In his season of burnout, he made a lot of decisions that were inconsistent with his values in an attempt to make himself feel less restless and help him snap out of his dark season. It can be tempting when you're suffering from burnout to go out and make similar reckless, huge life changes—to quit your job, buy a new house, get a divorce, take up bungee jumping (okay, so that last one might not be so bad). Just know that making those changes is unlikely to address the problem. Unfortunately, making sweeping changes during a time of stress usually just creates new problems. So like a pilot who has to be especially careful because one of his avionics sensors is malfunctioning, you need to be very careful because your consequence sensor is not functioning fully. You'll have to be especially careful about those big decisions.

Working Memory

If you have burnout brain, you'll likely struggle with reductions in something psychologists call working memory.[10] Our working memory is almost like a whiteboard for the brain, where we can keep relevant information stored until we don't need it anymore. So one of the things you're very likely to notice if you're struggling with burnout is that you often go to that whiteboard to grab a piece of information that you just stored there a moment ago, only to find that information erased.

For me, one indication that I'm struggling with this is when I find myself walking down a hallway toward someone's office at the church only to realize I don't remember what I'm meeting that person to talk about. Of course, that sort of thing happens to all of us from time to time. And it's important to know what's normal for you when it comes to those moments of forgetfulness. I know that I might normally have an experience like that once a month even when my brain is working as it should. But if I start having this experience every other day, I know something isn't right. By the way, this working memory thing is also related to attention. So if you find yourself drifting off when someone is talking to you, or you drive home and have the feeling that you just showed up at home and don't even really remember the drive, these are also indicators that burnout may be taking a toll.

What's Fight-or-Flight Got to Do with It?

While we're talking about brain parts and functions, let's talk a bit about the amygdala. Under that wrinkly gray carpet you usually picture when you think about the brain is a glob of really weird-looking pieces and parts that do specialized jobs, many of which are crucial to your survival. In that glob called the midbrain, there are two almond-shaped parts called the amygdalae. Each amygdala is involved in the process of interacting with your prefrontal cortex about emotions, with special attention given to the emotion of fear.[11,12] In fact, the amygdala is the part of your brain that is most involved with triggering the fight-or-flight mode in the brain and the rest of our bodies.[13]

So long as there is excellent connectivity and activity going on between the prefrontal cortex and the amygdala, we tend to make good decisions about whether to find situations threatening or nonthreatening. But remember that we said that when chronic stress is the norm, our prefrontal cortex doesn't function as effectively as it should, so the more reactive, emotional parts of our brain have freer rein to trigger panic when we should probably remain calm.

Worse, once we are triggered into fight-or-flight, the prefrontal cortex goes on a sort of mini-vacation. God designed us that way, so that the fastest, survival-based parts of our brain take charge when survival is the number one priority. One way to think of the prefrontal cortex in your brain is to think of it like a brilliant CEO of a large company. When you ask the brilliant CEO some major question about a problem no one else can solve, the CEO leans back in their chair and thinks for several minutes. It may seem like it's taking forever for them to think of something, but when they do speak, you realize why they get paid the big bucks. Their insight is brilliant. On the other hand, I tend to think of the amygdaloid bodies as that loss prevention guy at the company who is a little disheveled, has a dozen coffee stains on his tie, but his revolver is perfectly polished. This guy lives for escape routes and fire extinguisher inspections, and no one allows him to come to staff meetings because the only thing he knows how to say is "we're all gonna die."

But if the building really is on fire, you don't want to ask the CEO what to do. Because if you do, while the CEO sits back in their chair and thinks about it for ten minutes, everyone is going to die. In that life-and-death emergency, you need the loss prevention guy in charge. He may not be the most brilliant person on the org chart, but he is likely the person best suited to evacuate the building. On the other hand, complex problems call for the insight of the CEO. You need both people. But you want to make sure that you're involving the right person for the right job.

And here's where the rubber meets the road—chronic stress primes the pump for fight-or-flight responses and, as we've already said, handicaps our prefrontal cortex. So when chronic stress is the norm in your life, you're putting that loss prevention guy in the C suite to make the big calls. In my opinion, that's what happened to Mike Wallace (we talked about that in chapter 3), and it almost caused him to make a big call that cost him his life.

The Big Picture

As a researcher in the field of organizational psychology, I would make the case that there are three major components of a healthy job that, when in balance, provide a healthy and enjoyable work life: passion, people, and productivity. It is possible, of course, to be successful working at a job where you are not passionate about what you do. But if you're not passionate, the job will probably not be a joy for you. It will be something you do to collect a paycheck, and your heart will not be completely in it.

The best jobs are those that allow you to exercise your passion. Maybe you're passionate about helping people. If so, you may be very good at some sort of customer service role. And, so long as you are able to keep your passion connected to the daily tasks you have to do, you'll find joy in your job. Sure, there will be moments that agitate you, and, like any job, there will be frustrations and concerns along the way. But if you are passionate about what you do, you'll still enjoy getting up in the morning and going to work.

You also need connection, and that's where the people part comes in. Human interaction at work is an important part of what we need to be successful. I'm writing this book after the COVID-19 pandemic, and during that crisis, researchers like me learned a lot about work arrangements. Just about every sort of work situation has been tested since 2020, and we're learning a lot about different ways people can get their jobs done in nontraditional ways. But one thing we continue to learn is that people struggle to work in a vacuum of social interaction and support. While it is true that sometimes we can get more done when we're not distracted by others, our mental and emotional well-being is better when we have good relationships at work.

Finally, productivity is key, or else there is no point in work. We have to produce something of value, or there isn't really any point to showing up. Generally speaking, the company you work for will keep an eye on productivity. If it's taking a major hit, they'll let you know. However, we know that in battling burnout *there is a need for workers to see and feel good about their productivity.* There is a need for us to be able to take a step back from our work, admire it, and see the value in what we have accomplished.

This is especially important in fields where we aren't creating a physical product and we stare at computers all day. If you're a carpenter, you can step back from a room full of cabinets and admire your handiwork. If you're a sheet-metal worker in an aircraft factory, you can admire the section of the airplane that you built as it flies by. But if you're an accountant and you helped prepare hundreds of tax reports, it's not as easy to admire your work. Yet it's just as important to find a way to do that.

So here's the big picture: when you have burnout brain, you will begin to lose your passion for what you do. Even if it's something you really love, like medicine was for Harper, you can completely lose your turbo-charged love of writing, helping people, creating, building, preaching, teaching, public service, etc. And when that goes away, work will start to seem much more difficult and like a terrifying mountain to climb rather than an enjoyable challenge.

And, somewhere along the way, burnout brain will cause you to be less relational. We talked about that in chapter 5. You'll find yourself being sharp or withdrawn from people you used to engage with in a healthy way. You'll be more reactive and less emotionally aware. Struggling to regulate your impulses, you'll say things that you later wish you hadn't. In the end, you'll notice that the people at work who used to help bolster you up in difficult times are not around as much because they tend to duck down hallways when they see you coming.

Probably the last thing to go when we're dealing with burnout is productivity. Part of that is because we understand how crucial it is that we still produce at the level expected by our employer—no matter what we're going through. We don't want to lose our jobs. Still, when a major case of burnout sets in, eventually your productivity will drop. When that happens, it will not only create issues for you at work but will also create self-esteem issues for you. Perhaps even before your productivity losses are noticed by your bosses, you'll notice them. And you'll start to be anxious about where you stand at work.

For Harper, her passion is gone, the people aspect of her work has taken a beating, and she is starting to struggle with productivity. That's why she sits in her car before her shift, not wanting to start a moment early. She knows that things are not as they should be. She's dealing with that burnout brain thing in a big way.

Reengaging the *Why* and the *Who* to Get Your Occupational Life Back

If I were counseling Harper in the middle of her challenge with burnout, I would want her to pay attention to what we've already covered in this book regarding stress reduction and healthy life choices. In addition, I'd want her to reengage with her purpose (the *why*) and the people (the *who*) at work with whom she used to have healthy relationships.

Having observed how she's lost her passion for what she does, I would want her to engage with the why of her work again. What is it about this work that excited her in the first place? What was the driving passion that helped her survive years of medical school and her internship? What are some of the stories that she may remember of using her occupation to change people's lives? And, perhaps an even more important question, if she were to dream a little, what would she like to accomplish in this field? What would she like her legacy to be?

And then, in terms of reengaging with people, she may need to think about what has happened and what she's said to her co-workers in a spirit of burnout, and there may need to be some apologies. She may need to do some repair work to reestablish relationships with people who could really help her find her way at work again. Beyond this, she may need to work with a counselor or life coach who can help her work through some of the unhealthy relational habits she's developed in this burnout season so that she can exercise some new relational skills that will help those relationships to heal.

If you're following along and you're also trying to reengage the *why* and the *who*, let me encourage you to use a journal for this part. I know, I know—most of the folks I work with think that journaling is for scrapbookers who watch Hallmark movies and collect Precious Moments figurines, not for them. Trust me; journaling is much more powerful than you might think. When we're trying to figure out things in life, writing things down is one of the most powerful ways we can help our brain process and remember what we're learning. So take a moment and write down what you're remembering about your passion for what you do and what your dreams are moving forward. Write down what you're learning about your interactions with people and how you want to improve them. It will help.

Crafting a Better Work Environment

One thing we didn't talk about with Harper's situation is work environment. The way work environment and burnout are related is a topic that deserves a whole book. Work environment includes things like the physical environment around you (your desk, your chair, your lobby, your workstation, your workbench, etc.), but it also includes abstract things like your level of clarity about your job responsibilities, the way coworkers share the workload, and the extent to which you can be yourself at work. In most work environments, there will be things you can't change. But you want to focus on the things that you do have control over. Would it help to improve or change any of those things?

For some people it might be getting greater clarity about what you're supposed to do in certain situations at work. For others it might be requesting a chair that doesn't have a broken armrest.

Or it might be asking your employer if you can wear earplugs so that the background noise in the plant won't be as distracting from what you're trying to do. Regardless, empower yourself to do what you can to make your work environment better.

If you think you have no power to improve your work environment, double-check to make sure that's true. Sometimes a small adjustment can help, so don't sell yourself on the fact that you can't change anything. Be willing to try little things and see if they might make a big difference.

Why Shouldn't You Just Leave This Job and Start Over?

One of the most unpleasant feelings of burnout is restlessness. It's a feeling that tells you that you need to do something—anything—in order to feel joy. No matter what it costs. And when people have that sort of restless feeling related to their work, they're often tempted to quit their job and look for something completely different. I've seen it happen dozens of times. A person goes through a season of burnout, and instead of interpreting that season as a time to deal with unhealthy personal patterns and fight back against an unreasonable stress load, they interpret it as a sign they aren't in the right occupation anymore and leave their job.

I've made the point that rest is one of the most important recovery tools in your battle with burnout. Often these folks actually get several weeks of rest after leaving their job, and once a little sanity creeps back into their cortex, they realize that they really loved what they did. But, by then, they can't go back to the job they left. At that point they find themselves dealing with the stress of starting over, and they're right back in the high-stress lifestyle that they thought they were getting rid of.

Let me just encourage you not to make any *huge, life-altering decisions* in the middle of a burnout battle. Burnout brain is like a deep fog mentally, and in that fog, you're not going to see clearly enough to evaluate a change of direction or destination. Remind yourself that there is time to make course changes once you are in a healthier place and that the payoff for a better decision down the road is worth the price of being patient today. If you're in a situation where you may be forced to make a big decision about work in a season of burnout, you'll want to bring in trusted advisers who aren't fighting the fog of burnout brain. It would be better to get advice from people who can see clearly in this situation than to take a shot in the dark.

In the end, it's important to know that feelings come and go. You may feel today like you can't go on at this company, in this type of job, or doing this kind of work. Maybe those feelings will last and you'll need to make a permanent move. It's more likely, though, that what you're feeling right now is transient, and you will soon have feelings of wanting to stay. Here again, a journal helps a lot. Write down what those feelings are at both extreme swings of the pendulum. As you revisit what you've written, it will be easier to see the back and forth of your feelings, as well as the parts that stay consistent.

A Biblical Perspective

Remember that God assigned work before the fall of man. God gave Adam a job in the garden of Eden before sin entered the world and everything went sideways. That tells me that there is a divine aspect of work. There is an aspect of work that is part of God's perfect will, unspoiled by the influence of sin. Of course, we know from reading God's curse after the first sin that work became difficult as a side effect of sin.

I may be making too many assumptions here, but I think the divine aspect of work is achievement, creativity, and service. I think the curse of sin mixed exhaustion into the work experience. So it makes sense to me that if we want to have the best possible work experience, we need to fight exhaustion at work wherever we can. Sure, work will be tiring, but the more we can fight back against exhaustion and create a platform for achievement, creativity, and service, the more we can get back to the will of God in our work. We don't have to accept or normalize a zombie-like, going-through-the-motions, exhausted work life. We can insist on a passionate, joyful work life. And when we do, we are experiencing work as God designed it to be.

CHAPTER 7
Group Discussion Questions

1. How has stress impacted your feelings about and experience at work?

2. Do you identify with the concept of burnout brain? Have you ever dealt with that? What was that experience like?

3. Have you ever had to repair relationship damage that you accidentally did at work as a result of stress? How did you address the problem?

4. How important do you think a sense of purpose is at work? Is it possible to have a sense of purpose even about a job that you don't love?

5. Based on what you know about God from Scripture, what do you think God wants our work experience to be like?

Getting Your Life Back Navigationally

Burnout is a battle. But it is also a ready-made chance to get some perspective. In fact, I've come to believe that a season of burnout is often the price people pay for a chance to get unstuck in life. By that, I mean that *some of us are unlikely to stop going ninety miles per hour down the wrong road until we run out of gas.* When we do run out of gas, that forced stop gives us the chance to look around, take stock of our direction, and decide whether we want to keep driving down the same path. Sometimes a crisis is a blessing in disguise. In this chapter we'll talk about how to get your life back *navigationally* and make sure you're on the right path in life.

There are a couple reasons why it's important to make the most of this chance to evaluate your path.

1. Your Path Will Determine Your Destination

Next month I'll be getting on a plane to Nashville for a counseling conference. These days I fly a lot, and I'm pretty used to the routine.

I'm used to the little safety song and dance, the airplane crackers, the turbulence, the delays, the cancelations, the airport confusion . . . it's all becoming a familiar script to me now. I know what to expect. But suppose I get on that plane to Nashville, and after landing, the pilot gets on the intercom and says, "Hey, folks, I hate to tell you this . . . man this is so embarrassing . . . I know we were supposed to end up at Nashville International, but somehow we just landed at Dallas Fort Worth International Airport in Texas. We're up here trying to figure this out. We aren't sure how we ended up here." That would be a new experience. Usually, if you land somewhere other than what your ticket says, you get plenty of explanations for why that's the case. There are weather problems, or there's some issue at the airport where you were heading. But "we don't know why" would be an interesting excuse. It's not one I've ever heard.

Were that to ever happen, my hunch is that all of us sitting in the plane would have no trouble explaining to the pilot what had actually happened. It's not that complicated. At some point, the plane became oriented toward DFW. The plane ended up where the plane was pointed. It's physically impossible for the plane to follow a path to Nashville and end up in Dallas. Chances are, we ended up in Dallas because the navigational equipment of the plane was set to Dallas. Your destination is the result of your navigation. It's that simple.

I've sat across from so many people in my counseling work who have explained where they ended up in life, only to tell me they have no idea how they ended up there. One of those people was the person I mentioned in chapter 1. Remember the guy I talked to on the plane? As you may recall, he was dealing with all sorts of burnout-related life choices that had created issues for him in nearly every area of his life. His connection with his kids was falling apart. His marriage was in trouble. He was starting to have problems at work, even though work was almost all he had to lean on at that point in his life. He really felt the walls closing in on him. And I recall him saying, *"I don't know how I ended up here."* I didn't push him hard on this point at the time because I truly think he was in the middle of a crisis, and this is some heavy truth to embrace. But the truth is that he ended up there because that's where his internal navigator was pointed.

Somewhere deep down, his navigator was pointed toward success at all costs, and he was arriving at his destination. He was successful, but it had cost him far more than he would have initially bargained for. The good news is that navigation, by definition, is changeable. Just as a pilot can make the decision to change destinations by turning a few knobs in the cockpit and reorienting the navigation systems so that they follow a new path, you can do the same thing with your life. It's never too late.

2. Your Path Becomes a Guide over Time

I've gotten into woodworking in the last couple of years. For me, it's one of those restful activities we talked about earlier. I'm still new to the craft, and I'm learning the basics. One thing I really wanted to be able to do was hand cut dovetail joints when making wooden boxes, drawers, or other furniture. In order to cut dovetails, you have to be scary precise with your handsaw. That saw has to cut along just the right line, or the joint won't fit together properly.

When I was learning to do this, the instructor made a big point about how important the first few strokes of the saw were. He said, "Those first strokes start your kerf, and your kerf will take charge of the cut." The kerf is the cut itself—the path that the saw creates as it moves through the wood. He was saying that once that cut was established, the sides of the cut would start guiding the saw down the same path.

It's just like choosing a path in life. In the early days of your adult life, your family life, your career, or your spiritual journey, you take initial steps that begin to form a path. Then, after a little while, the path starts to take on a life of its own, and it exerts pressure on your future choices and steps.

So often in this book I've used the metaphor of being on autopilot for what it's like to deal with burnout. To think of another image to represent this, in many areas of our life, burnout happens or gets worse because we are bearing up under the stress of life by letting the ruts in the road tell us which next step we should take and ending up further down a road that, if we were honest with ourselves, might not be best.

So if you're dealing with burnout, one of the benefits of the forced slowdown you're dealing with may be the opportunity to take stock of the paths you're on to make sure they're the right ones. In this chapter we're addressing the importance of being healthy *navigationally*—choosing healthy paths for yourself. And we'll be talking about your paths in three key areas: your habits, priorities, and relationship with God.

Habits

Few things influence our daily choices as much as habits. Our habits have a lot to do with when we wake up in the morning, what we have for breakfast, how we handle the drive to work, how we interact with coworkers, how we do our work, when we wrap up our workday, whether we call our spouse on the way home, what we do when we first get home, when we decide to eat dinner, whether we eat with the family, what we eat for dinner, what we do in our downtime, what we do to get ready for bed, and when we actually go to sleep. And I just hit the highlights here. Habits are a factor in what we do and how we do things in nearly every waking moment of our lives. That's not a bad thing. This is a power that can be constructive or destructive. It's your choice.

People who use the power of habit for good become pros at two important tasks. First, they learn to become *aware* of their habits and routines. Second, they learn how to *adjust* their habits to get better outcomes. So how do you do those two things? You will start to develop awareness of your habits when you begin to take stock of what you do mindlessly. Try this: sit down with a piece of paper and just write down the different things you did today without thinking. Chances are, you'll end up with a very long list very quickly. Then, take some time to think about whether or not you're happy with the outcomes of those automatic routines.

I'll give it a try here:

This morning, I woke up later than I intended to. That's a bad habit of mine that solidified during the COVID pandemic; it's easy for me to sleep past when I meant to wake up. And, rather than showering, shaving, putting on some nice cologne, and dressing up nice, I did the minimum hygiene things, threw on some clothes, and headed out for the day. I told my wife what my plans were for this morning and kissed her goodbye on the way out. In a way, that wasn't something I did without thinking. I did feel a real sense of connection with Wendy on my way out of the house. She's been praying for me a lot lately, and she cares a lot about my writing and my work. I definitely felt her love and encouragement. That wasn't an autopilot thing. And yet the hello-goodbye thing is kind of a habit that we've developed over the years. That's a good habit—one I'm very happy about. I'm glad we connect in those arrival and departure moments.

Then, instead of eating something healthy for breakfast, I stopped at the fast-food restaurant where I've bought breakfast a million times and ordered the same old greasy breakfast I've eaten there so many times before. After that, I drove to the university library where I've been writing most of this book over the past couple of weeks.

In evaluating what I did this morning by habit, I definitely see a lot of room for improvement. Today is a big day. Hopefully I will finish writing the book that you're reading today. I could have done a much better job giving today a great start. I could have made the decision to wake up on time and overridden my sleeping-in habit. I could have made the decision to take the time to do all the hygiene and grooming things that make you feel like a million bucks when you leave the house. And I could have eaten a healthy breakfast. That would have required *adjusting* my habits, but if I had made those adjustments, imagine how much better today might have gone.

The most successful people out there understand that habits are like recipes. If you have (and correctly follow) a great recipe, all the cookies you bake will be great. And you may end up baking a lot of cookies. On the other hand, if you have a lousy recipe, all the cookies you bake will be lousy.

So this is a chance in your life to open up the recipe box and evaluate the habits you've normalized over the years. It's a great chance to ask yourself how happy you are with how the cookies are turning out and decide whether or not it's time to make some changes to the recipe.

And, while you're evaluating your habits, it might be worthwhile to think about your spiritual habits as well. In seasons of stress, the habits you've developed in your relationship with God will become especially important.

For many of us, the story of Daniel in the lions' den has been a favorite since childhood. It's really amazing to think of God sending an angel to shut the mouths of the lions that would otherwise have torn Daniel apart and had him for dinner. The moral of the story is that God protected Daniel because he did the right thing. But what was that right thing again? It was that he still prayed to God, even though the king of Persia (who was indirectly Daniel's boss, by the way) had decreed that no one could pray to anyone, human or divine, other than him. But Daniel prayed to the true God anyway. That's why he ended up in the lions' den, and Daniel's devotion to following God and doing the right thing is why God protected him in that situation.

But don't run too quickly past the verse where the Bible tells us that Daniel prayed when he was told not to:

> But when Daniel learned that the law had been signed, he went home and knelt down *as usual* in his upstairs room, with its windows open

toward Jerusalem. He prayed three times a day, *just as he had always done*, giving thanks to his God.

Daniel 6:10, emphasis added

The phrases "as usual" and "just as he had always done" are there to emphasize that praying to God was, for Daniel, a matter of well-established habit. So when things got tough and he was under pressure not to do the right thing, there was just as much pressure from the power of habit to do what he knew he should do. That's the thing: in life there will be moments when the pressure is on, and what you do in those moments will be crucial for your life path. But what you do in those moments will be radically influenced by the habits you've established before the heat is on.

The questions I would encourage you to ask yourself are these:

Am I aware of the habits that influence my life every day?
Am I happy with the outcome of these habits?
Which good habits do I need to celebrate and reinforce?
Which bad habits do I need to rethink and replace?
How will I make those changes?

Priorities

One of the messages I've been hammering home in this book since chapter 1 is that you are a finite person with finite resources. It is possible to exhaust your time, finances, energy, emotional well-being, and relationship capital. And anytime you have limited resources and seemingly unlimited demands and opportunities to spend, it pays to start budgeting.

Years ago, I sat across from a very sweet couple who were in crisis. We'll call him Dave, and we'll call her Sheila. He was one of the most burned-out people I've ever talked to. As Sheila explained all of Dave's commitments to me, his intense burnout began to make sense. Here was a guy who said yes to everything. He had a full-time commission job where there was really no time clock. When others would ask him to cover their shifts so they could be gone for this reason or that, he never said no. Dave always said yes. Unless he made more sales during those extra shifts, he didn't make any more money, but at least he was popular with everyone he subbed for. When his boss needed someone to organize a birthday party or other workplace celebration, Dave seemed to always be the one tapped for the job.

Having had some background in construction when he was younger, Dave had been asked to help with rebuilding part of one of the buildings at the private school where his kids attended. He said yes to that, too. And not too long after he said yes to that commitment, he was asked to join the board of the homeowners association in his neighborhood. I can't recall how many other commitments the guy had—those are the ones I remember this many years hence. Anyhow, one night the homeowners association president called Dave and let him know that the lawn service company they had hired to cut the grass at the entrance to the neighborhood had canceled on them, and since Dave was the only person on the association board with a riding mower, they were hoping he could cut the grass just this one time.

Sheila rolled over in bed about eleven that night to discover that Dave wasn't there. She called him on his cell phone and found out that he was trying to cut the grass at that late hour because he had figured out there was no other time he had available to do it. Sheila was cross with him, and that's reasonable. Her husband was so overcommitted they didn't have much of a relationship anymore. And she missed him. Perhaps it didn't come out in the best way, but she was feeling like there was no Dave left over for her after all the rest of his commitments were taken care of.

For Dave, his burnout crisis happened at roughly eleven-fifteen, sitting on a riding mower in the dark, being eaten alive by mosquitos, staring off into space, and realizing that no matter how many things he did, and no matter how good his intentions were, he was still disappointing the person who mattered most to him.

By the time I met with Dave and Sheila, he was depressed and disconnected, not feeling like he could meet *any* of his commitments, much less all of them. At the time, he needed more help than I could provide, and I referred him to a skilled therapist. Eventually, he came back to see me when he was doing better, and we discussed his need to prioritize. It was part of what he needed to do to get his life back on track navigationally.

Here's the exercise I did with him. I took a piece of paper and wrote "24 hours" at the top of the page. Then I asked him about different commitments he had and how much time he spent on each on an average day. Here's what it looked like:

Time I can spend	24 hours
Sleep/waking routine/grooming	8 hours
Work and work commute	9 hours
Must-do tasks (like getting the oil changed or going to the grocery store)	2 hours
Dinner and time with kids	2 hours
Homeowners association	1 hour
Time helping kids with homework	1 hour
Time watching TV/on the internet/working from home	3 hours
Hobby/free time	1 hour
	-3 hours

When we charted Dave's normal day, he was overcommitted by three hours, and just think of how many things happen every day that we didn't list here that still take up time! The reason the guy ended up in my office looking like he had completely checked out was that he was finishing every day in a deficit situation. By the way, notice that nowhere on this chart is time for Sheila. And nowhere on this chart is any kind of intentional time for God. And even with those huge gaps, he's still ending every day with a negative balance. Eventually that kind of life will catch up with you. Dave will never forget the night it caught up with him while he was sitting on that riding mower.

Prioritizing your life is what you do when you realize you can't keep normalizing a daily deficit. At some point you have to make peace with that twenty-four-hour daily cap. And, accepting the fact that you will probably always have more demands on your life than you have hours in the day, one of the most powerful things you can do is decide where you want to spend the first and best of your time and energy, where you will give the rest of your time (the leftovers), and where you will have to say no and walk away.

Informally, at the church where I work, we have a culture of resource budgeting that goes like this: we separate opportunities into two categories—the "must" category and the "would be nice" category. Anything that doesn't fit into either of those two categories is a "no." I find that this is a helpful way of developing your own personal time-and-resources budget as well.

Try this exercise: take out a piece of paper and draw one column that you label "musts." There, fill in the demands and opportunities in life where you are unwilling to compromise. You will only want to put something in this column if you are truly willing to let other things fall through the cracks so as not to drop the ball in this area. It shouldn't be a very long list. And there should be people's names on the list. If tasks are the only things on the "must" list, you may need to go back and reread the chapter on getting your life back relationally.

Then draw a column labeled "would be nice" and write in all the things that you'd like to do if you had time. Then, order both lists from most important to least. Now, in the spirit of evaluating your path, ask yourself, *What would it take for me to budget my days to live out the priorities I've just outlined here?*

It might require a major life shift. But in all my years of counseling, I've never had someone come see me to lament the costs of putting their family first, or of letting go of a too-many-commitments lifestyle in favor of a focused, keep-the-main-thing-the-main-thing lifestyle. My hunch is that every bit of effort you spend to prioritize your life with wisdom and intentionality will pay huge dividends in the long run.

Relationship with God

I saved the best navigational guidance for last. Here's what the Bible says about making sure you're on the right path: "Trust in the LORD with all your heart; do not depend on your own understanding. Seek his will in all you do, and *he will show you which path to take*" (Proverbs 3:5–6, emphasis added).

It's an awesome thought that the all-knowing God of the universe is willing to show us which path we should take in this stressful world. But in order to cash in on that offer, we need to do three things: trust God with all our heart, don't depend on our own understanding, and seek his will in everything we do. Let's break it down.

Trust God with All Your Heart

I think Solomon wants to emphasize the idea of trusting in God with *all our heart* because it is human nature to trust in God with *some of our heart*. Often our paths in life look really weird because part of our loyalty is to money, success, or fame, and part of our loyalty is to the Lord. James had something to say about that kind of path:

> Be sure that your faith is in God alone. Do not waver, for a person with divided loyalty is as unsettled as a wave of the sea that is blown and tossed by the wind. Such people should not expect to receive anything from the Lord. Their loyalty is divided between God and the world, and they are unstable in everything they do.
>
> James 1:6–8

James is telling us that a person who wants to be loyal to God and to the trappings of this world at the same time is going to have a very unstable and unproductive life path. The deal on the table is this: God will show us the right path (usually a step at a time—God doesn't often give out entire maps) if we are willing to orient all of our loyalty toward him. And, for many of us, a path of undivided loyalty to God would look different from the one we're on. But imagine the simplicity of a life with that kind of singular focus!

Don't Depend on Your Own Understanding

When I was in middle school, an aircraft engineer came to speak to our science class. Wichita, Kansas, is a major player in the aviation manufacturing world, and the guy who came to talk to us was a top-notch engineering guy from Boeing. He gave a talk about the importance of instrumentation on the big jets, and he showed us how unreliable our senses could be when it comes to motion in flight.

Because I don't get motion sick, I volunteered for his little demonstration. I sat in a chair that spun, and I was supposed to say when I was spinning and in which direction while keeping my eyes closed. At a few points I heard the class laughing, and it turned out they were laughing because I was sure I was spinning in one direction or another after my chair had stopped turning. The engineer then began to talk about how pilots can get into situations in low visibility where their body tells them one thing, but the reality is something else entirely. It's in cases like those, he said, when a pilot's training to trust his instruments is crucial. In those moments, you have to make a hard choice. You have to decide whether to trust the instruments or go with your gut.

I think Solomon was trying to tell us that when you're trying to make difficult decisions in complex situations, you will have to make the same hard decision. You'll often be aware of what God says you should do and what you feel like you should do. Sometimes those things match and the decision is easy. But a lot of the time your feelings will tell you to do something different from what you know God would want you to do. It is in those moments that you'll have to decide whether to depend on your gut or on your God. The key thing to remember is that your gut can be unreliable. But if you depend on God, he has promised to show you the right path. Just like that pilot in limited visibility, you have to trust that something else is more reliable than your feelings. Once you come to accept that, you can fly in any weather.

Seek His Will in Everything You Do

I'm blessed to have the most wonderful grandparents ever; they are with the Lord now, and I look forward to seeing them again one day in heaven. For now, I'm blessed with sweet memories of interacting with them when I was younger. My dad's dad was the pastor of the same church in Fort Worth, Texas, for almost fifty years, and then he came and served as care pastor at our church for over ten years.

One of the things I remember most about my grandpa was his desire to pray about everything. He would stop you in the middle of nearly any conversation on any topic in order to pray with you about it. I remember one day I was getting ready to leave after a visit with my grandpa, and he asked me where I was going next. I told him I was going to buy a tie to wear at a wedding I would be officiating. I'll never forget him stopping me mid-sentence to pray with me that I would find the right tie and that *it would be on sale*! I did, by the way, and it was. My grandpa believed that God wanted to be involved in even the smallest, most mundane parts of his life. He was grateful for that, and he wanted to ask God for direction, even if it was about something as trivial as which tie to buy at the department store.

As you examine your paths, it's important to remember that even the small, seemingly insignificant paths of your life matter to God. Give him a seat at that table. You might be surprised at how exciting it can be to see God empower the simple and routine parts of your life with his purpose and power. Once you start asking God for guidance with the small things, you'll wonder why you didn't start doing that a long time ago.

You Can Always Carve Out a New Path

The most important thing to remember when you are doing the hard work of getting your life back navigationally is to remember that you always have the power to course correct. Never let yourself believe the lie that there's no point in charting a new path forward. The Bible has a special word for course correcting. It's called *repentance*. Repentance is all about looking at your current path, seeing where it hasn't been productive and pleasing to God, and making a choice to go down a different path. And it's never too late to repent. Just like the father who ran to the prodigal son to embrace him as he traveled the path home, God will run to embrace you if you choose to chart a course that follows him.

CHAPTER 8
Group Discussion Questions

1. Have you ever felt lost in life—like you didn't really know where you were headed, or like you were headed in the wrong direction? How did you get back on track?

2. We spent a lot of time talking about priorities. How do you manage your priorities to make sure the most important things get the first and best of you?

3. We mentioned that most of us don't really have enough time in our lives to do everything. What are some of the time consumers in your life that you would never sacrifice, and what are some time consumers that you're thinking you might need to let go of?

4. We talked about trusting God with *all* your heart and that it's important to do that intentionally because it is human

nature to trust God with only *some* of our heart. Has there ever been a situation in your life when you knew you were trusting God alone to help you with something stressful? What happened in that situation? What did you learn?

5. Is there an area of your life where you feel stuck in a rut? What would it take to start carving out a new path in that area?

A Good Game Plan for Today

At the beginning of this book I told the story of a fellow I met on an airplane who was experiencing burnout. And while I remember talking to him about how his life was being impacted personally, emotionally, relationally, spiritually, occupationally, and navigationally, I don't recall what, if anything, I told him he should do right away to start making progress in his burnout battle. Years have now passed, and I've studied burnout a great deal since that airplane conversation. Now I'd like to think I could give him some good here's-what-to-do-right-now kind of guidance. The moment has passed, so I can't do that for him. But I'd like to do that for you.

1. See Your Doctor

True, it's not the first time in this book I've suggested that you see your physician, but it bears mentioning again. As we established in chapter 3, burnout impacts you physically. You need to have a medical professional keep an eye on your physical health. I would recommend that you make an appointment to talk to your doctor about any symptoms of burnout you've been experiencing and to get a full physical. Make sure to let your doctor know if you've observed major diet changes, weight changes, recurring aches and pains, muscle cramps or tension, trouble sleeping, or any of the other physical symptoms mentioned in chapter 3.

Seeing the doctor can serve a few very important purposes. As I mentioned before, physical symptoms without diagnosable causes can be a fairly common feature of burnout, and reasonably so. It makes sense that if your body is dealing with substantial negative changes as the result of stress, you may become very aware of the fact that something just doesn't feel right. Seeing the doctor and having a thorough examination and some basic tests may help set your mind at ease if you find yourself obsessing over your physical health. On the other hand, if you are dealing with some sickness or undiagnosed problem that is compounding your stress and making your battle with burnout worse, it pays to know about it. So having your doctor check you out is a good thing, whether or not they find any problems.

It also pays to talk to someone who knows what they're talking about. I find that most physicians I meet are extremely well versed in the effects of stress on the body. So your physician is probably an excellent source of information about whether you should consider symptoms you've noticed to be a normal outcome of stress or to be caused by something else. If you and your doctor have a great rapport, that's fantastic, but make sure to get the benefit of their expertise. Resist the temptation to talk about the weather and who you think will make it to the Super Bowl. Take that appointment time as an opportunity to learn from someone who really knows their stuff. They can help you sort out what stress is doing to your body.

When you meet with your doctor, be prepared to take notes, and promise yourself you won't let your doctor's guidance go in one ear and out the other. If your doctor suggests going on a diet, give that diet the old college try. If your doctor suggests steps to lower your blood pressure, make it a priority to take those steps. And if your doctor tells you that you need to reduce your workload because stress is breaking you down, resist the temptation to nod and smile and then forget what she said.

Doctor's orders are doctor's orders. I know we don't use that term very much in today's culture, but years ago people used to talk about doctor's orders as if they were something sacred. The reason they talked about them that way was because there was trust and good faith that if the doctor told you to do something, it was for the best, and you should insist on giving it your best shot. So long as you have a great doctor (and most of us do), I think there's a lot of wisdom in having respect for doctor's orders.

2. See a Counselor

If you've never been to a counselor or therapist before, I understand that you may bristle a little bit at the idea of paying money to sit down and talk to a stranger about very personal, private challenges. So let me try to explain why I think it's a good idea to do just that. If you see a licensed counselor or therapist, you will be sitting across from someone who has been trained to listen to your experience, care about what you are going through, help you process that experience, and help you decide what you want to do next and how you want to do it.

Sure, therapy can be expensive, and it can be slightly awkward at first. I'll give you that. But in the long run, having a professional take time to help you slow down and process your experiences in a way that helps you get clarity and find peace is worth it. Most of us are already seeking counsel. Often we use our friends, spouses, or coworkers as informal therapists, but that's a fairly major burden to put on someone who wasn't trained for the job. Seeing a counselor may be a relief for both you and the people you already trust to give you counsel. They may need a bit of a break.

Perhaps you're reading this right now and thinking that this idea of getting therapy is *definitely not for you*. Often these kinds of thoughts come from the idea that if a person gets counseling it proves that they are in some way broken or weak. If that's how you feel, you are right—in a way. People who go to counseling are broken and weak. But so are people who don't go to counseling.

The Bible tells us that we are all broken: we have a sin nature. And we are definitely all weak compared to the strength we would like to have. But Paul reminds us in 2 Corinthians 12:10 that it is when we embrace our brokenness and weakness that we have the opportunity to lean into God's strength. So, yes, if you go to counseling, you might be uncomfortably up close and personal with your weaknesses, but that might actually put you on a trajectory to live a stronger life than you've ever lived before. That's why I say therapy is worth a shot.

3. See Your Pastor

I know that some folks reading this book might not be believers or churchgoers, so the idea of meeting with a pastor might not be something you want to add to your list. Let me encourage you, though, not to unilaterally rule out the idea. You might be surprised by how helpful it could be. I've met with and counseled several people who weren't believers or members of my church who were going through burnout. I'd like to think I was able to help them, both with their burnout journey and with their spiritual needs.

If you do have a home church, parish, or synagogue, I would recommend that you make an appointment to talk to your pastor, priest, or rabbi. Remember that while your physical and emotional wellness are important, you are more than your body and more than your brain. The most important part of you is your immortal soul. Talking to someone who is primarily concerned with your spiritual condition is a good idea when you're feeling the burden of stress weighing you down.

4. Turn Your Intentions into Action Plans

One of the things I've learned from dealing with people suffering from burnout is that they often already know several things they should be doing. They know they should be taking care of their body, so they've been meaning to go to the gym. They have a membership, of course, but they haven't been in a long time. They've been meaning to get their diet under control, but it's been difficult with their schedule and daily demands. They've been meaning to delegate work tasks to people on their team, but sometimes it feels easier just to do everything themselves. They've been meaning to prioritize their family and friendships, but this season has just been so busy they haven't been able to do that.

I'm working on this personally, and it's something I don't have mastered. I'm great at making plans for what I need to do to deal with challenges I experience in life. I'm just not necessarily great at following through with those plans. But this much I've learned: the only way to turn good intentions into realities is to come up with a solid action plan. Ask yourself what would have to happen if you were going to make this life change a sustainable, solid part of your lifestyle. What would you need to clear off your calendar? How would your thinking need to change? What distractions would threaten to undo your progress? Something like the following worksheet may prove helpful.

C—the CHANGE I want to make is

_____

H—here's HOW I think I can make this change part of my lifestyle

_____

A—the kind of ATTITUDE I need in order to stick with this is

N—the NEGATIVE influences/thought patterns I need to avoid are

G—the big-picture GOAL this change will help me achieve is

E—this is who or what will help me stay ENGAGED when I want to give up

5. Reduce and Refine

This is a concept I've used for a number of years with those I've counseled. We call it *reducing the unnecessary* and *refining the clumsy*. The idea behind it is that there are a lot of stressors each of us have in our daily lives that we could just excise. Some of them are abstract, like stressing over what a coworker thinks of you or stressing over whether you are a success. Others are much more concrete. For instance, sometimes reducing the unnecessary means saying no to elective opportunities that present themselves for extra work or stress. No matter how much you might want to take on that extra work, if it turns out to be the last straw, it's not worth it. Reducing your stress load is one of the first steps you should take if you're stuck in burnout and hoping to find your way out.

Refining the clumsy means looking at the things you must do and making sure you're doing them in the most effective and expeditious way. Perhaps one of your work tasks could be done much faster with a different software, or maybe there's a better way to delegate tasks to your team. Adjusting how you do what you must do is a great way to reduce what seems like unavoidable stress.

6. Revisit Your Purpose

If you hang around a person who is going through a dark season of burnout, one of the things you'll tend to notice is that they have a sort of fatalistic view of life. They tend to think of themselves as being like a hamster on a wheel, going through the motions and trying to function while concluding that there really is no point to this. They feel that way because burnout tends to rob us of our sense of purpose.

It happened to King Solomon. Solomon was the third king of Israel and a very wise person. And for a season, he was a very productive and driven individual. If you read the book of Proverbs, you will see how idealistic and driven young Solomon was. But when you get to the book of Ecclesiastes, burned-out Solomon insists that life is meaningless. He spends most of the book complaining about how life isn't fair and reiterating that there is no point in trying anymore.

I think God let us see that book of Solomon's self-talk so we would have a clear picture of what burnout really looks like. No matter how much stuff Solomon acquired, no matter how many achievements he had on his résumé, and no matter how intelligent he became, he still found himself numb, burned out, and reaching for something he couldn't find, saying, "Though I have searched repeatedly, I have not found what I was looking for" (Ecclesiastes 7:28).

Some translations say that Solomon said that his *soul* had repeatedly searched for something but hadn't found it. Personally, I think Solomon was dealing with the loss of purpose. Even with all his stuff, all his money, all his women, and all his wisdom, he still wasn't sure what he was supposed to accomplish in this world. So he threw up his hands in surrender and concluded that nothing matters.

In this, my last bit of guidance to share in this book, I would encourage you to throw your hands up in surrender, yes, but not in a defeated surrender like Solomon. There's a better kind of surrender.

Years ago, I was living in Oklahoma, and our local mall had a play area for small children. One day as I passed the play area, I noticed a little boy who clearly hoped to make his way in to play. I watched him as he looked at the slides and play equipment longingly, wishing he could be having fun with the other kids. Unfortunately for him, his parents were talking to some other adults and weren't helping him make it through the childproofed entrance. I watched him as he tried to climb into the play area and couldn't do it on his own. I watched him as he tried to figure out the latch to the play area door—a device that was clearly beyond his mastery. Then I watched him finally make his way back to his parents. He lifted his arms up, but his arms weren't lifted up in the surrender of defeat. They were lifted up in the surrender of trust. The little boy trusted that when he reached up, his dad would scoop him up in his arms and lift him over the barrier and help him arrive where he needed to be.

I'm encouraging you to reach your arms up to your heavenly father in the surrender of trust, knowing that he sees the barriers that have caused you so much stress and exhaustion. He cares about your pain and frustration. And he can pick you up and place you where you need to be. It is my prayer that he will do that for you.

ACKNOWLEDGMENTS

I started thinking about writing this book thirteen years ago, and **my wife, Wendy**, was the first person I told about it. Over those thirteen years, she was my constant supporter as I did tons of research, completed two graduate degrees, and began studying burnout academically. She was there to encourage me when publishers turned the book idea down, and she was there to celebrate with me years later when Bethany House committed to making this book a reality. She has always believed in me, and without her, this book would never have been written. She is my person. I am so thankful for her.

My daughters, Cheyenne and Summer, are a constant source of joy, and they love me enough to listen to my ramblings about burnout and chronic stress. That's a lot of love. I've learned a lot from them, and I hope this book will be a blessing for their generation.

This book is dedicated to **my dad, Mark Hoover**. Along with **my mom, Mary Alice**, he championed this project from day one, and his transparency about his own experience helped me understand burnout at a deep level.

I am blessed to serve **the family of NewSpring Church** as associate pastor. In the thirteen years I've served in that role, I've been extravagantly loved and supported by this amazing group of people. At every stage of this book project I was prayed for and encouraged by NewSpringers, and I felt the energy of their support all along the way.

At **Regent University**, I serve as an assistant professor and the director of the master of science in general psychology program. I am so proud to be associated with a school that stands for excellence in academic pursuit and unapologetic loyalty to Christ. While I was completing this book, our founder and chancellor, Dr. M. G. (Pat) Robertson, went home to be with the Lord. I wish to honor Dr. Robertson for his years of dedication to our fine school.

Dr. Les Parrott has been a wonderful friend and mentor over the past decade. His guidance in the early days of crafting the idea for the book was invaluable. And I am so blessed that he was willing to write the foreword. Les has helped me grow as a writer and a speaker, and I will always be in his debt.

Dr. Anna Ord is my go-to resource for all things neuropsychology. In addition to this, she serves as the dean of my department at Regent University. I have been greatly blessed by her leadership and contribution to this project.

Dr. Jed Holmes (MD, retired) is the most talented physician I have ever known. I am fortunate that he happens to live in Kansas and I was able to dialogue with him about the chapter titled "Getting Your Life Back Physically." Jed reviewed the chapter and offered his insight. I am very thankful for his help with the book.

Janet Kobobel Grant is my literary agent. I pitched a version of this book to her back in 2015, so it's been a long road. I appreciate Janet's dedication to finding just the right home for this project and her continued encouragement through the process.

I have been humbled and amazed by the enthusiasm for this project that **the entire team at Bethany House Publishers** has shown. They have encouraged me by catching the vision for this project and pursuing that vision with excellence and dedication. I especially want to thank my editor Andy McGuire, who has helped me navigate the challenges of being a first-time author.

Finally, it's important that I say that any good thing that comes from this book should be credited to **Jesus Christ**. God is the source of personal transformation, and any glory from this project should go to him.

PERSON Chart

Today's date _____

If we want to truly understand our success level in life, we must consider all the different areas of living that are important to us. The goal of this chart is to help provide a sort of wide-angle view of how you are feeling about major dimensions of your life experience on a daily basis.

In a few sentences, write a description about what your day was like. Be sure to include major stressors or draining events and major relaxers or energizing events.

_____

_____

_____

_____

_____

Now score each of the following areas of your life on a scale of 1–10. Here's how to do that: score the item a 10 if you felt as well as you can imagine a person possibly feeling in that category, and a 1 if you felt as bad as you can imagine a person feeling. Score a 5 if you felt completely neutral in that category for the day (i.e., I didn't feel good, but I didn't feel bad).

P	E	R	S	O	N
PHYSICAL Health	EMOTIONAL Wellbeing	RELATIONAL Connectedness	SPIRITUAL Transcendence	OCCUPATIONAL Performance	NAVIGATIONAL Contentment

Spiritual Transcendence = The level of closeness I feel to God, and the level to which my belief in God helped me find significance and meaning in my daily struggles.

Navigational Contentment = The level of my confidence that I am moving in the right direction in life, that I have some control over the outcomes of my endeavors, and that I will be successful in the future.

NOTES

Foreword by Les Parrott

1. "Burn-out an 'occupational phenomenon': International Classification of Diseases," World Health Organization, Mary 28, 2019, https://www.who .int/news/item/28-05-2019-burn-out-an-occupational-phenomenon-inter national-classification-of-diseases.

2. "Addressing Employee Burnout: Are You Solving the Right Problem?" McKinsey Health Institute, May 27, 2022, https://www.mckinsey.com/mhi /our-insights/addressing-employee-burnout-are-you-solving-the-right -problem.

3. Ashley Abramson, "Burnout and Stress Are Everywhere," January 1, 2022, American Psychological Association, *Monitor on Psychology* 53, no. 1 (January 2022), https://www.apa.org/monitor/2022/01/special-burnout-stress.

Chapter 1: Nietzsche or Goldilocks?

1. Amy F. T. Arnsten, "Stress Signalling Pathways that Impair Prefrontal Cortex Structure and Function," *Nature Reviews Neuroscience* 10, no. 6 (2009): 414–416, https://doi.org/10.1038/nrn2648 and Simon L. Dolan, *De-Stress at Work: Understanding and Combatting Chronic Stress*, 1st ed., vol. 1. (United Kingdom: Routledge, 2023), 87–88.

2. William R. Lovallo, *Stress and Health: Biological and Psychological Interactions*, 3rd ed. (Los Angeles: SAGE Publications, Inc, 2016), chapters 3–7.

3. Annemiek J. Roete, Marije Elferink-Gemser, Ruby T. A. Otter, Inge K. Stoter, and Robert P. Lamberts, "A Systematic Review on Markers of Functional Overreaching in Endurance Athletes," *International Journal of Sports Physiology and Performance* 16, no. 8 (2021): 1065–1073.

4. Luana C. Main and Grant J. Landers, "Overtraining Or Burnout: A Training and Psycho-Behavioural Case Study," *International Journal of Sports Science & Coaching* 7, no. 1 (2012): 24–25; Romain Meeusen, "The Overtraining Syndrome: Diagnosis and Management," in *The Olympic Textbook of Medicine in Sport* (Oxford, UK: Wiley-Blackwell, 2008), 138–59, [this entire chapter is a good resource to explain overtraining] and Lovallo, *Stress and Health*, 71.

Chapter 2: Super Rats

1. Hans Selye, *The Stress of Life*, 2nd ed. (New York: McGraw-Hill, 1978), 112–13 and Dolan, *De-Stress at Work*, p. 31.

2. Hans Selye, "A Syndrome Produced by Diverse Nocuous Agents," *Nature* (London) 138, no. 3479 (1936): 32–32, https://doi.org/10.1038/138032a0.

3. Selye, *The Stress of Life*, pp. 112–13. Fortunately, over time, the field of social science research has developed far better understanding of animal research ethics. While I mention this experiment because the findings have value, I am aware of and sensitive to the ethical implications of this sort of old-school psychological animal research.

4. Selye, *The Stress of Life* [this book is nearly completely about the alarm-adaptation-exhaustion process] and Lovallo, *Stress and Health*, 35–36 [general adaptation syndrome, alarm, adaptation, exhaustion].

5. Christina Maslach, "Burned-out," *Human Behavior* 5, no. 9 (1976): 16–22.

6. Chloé Meredith, Wilmar Schaufeli, Charlotte Struyve, Machteld Vandecandelaere, Sarah Gielen, and Eva Kyndt, "'Burnout Contagion' among Teachers: A Social Network Approach," *Journal of Occupational and Organizational Psychology* 93, no. 2 (2020): 328–52, https://doi.org/10.1111/joop.12296.

7. Christina Maslach, W. B. Schaufeli, and M. P. Leiter, "Job Burnout," *Annual Review of Psychology* 52, (2001): 402, https://doi.org/10.1146/annurev.psych.52.1.397.

8. Robert S. Stawski, David M. Almeida, Margie E. Lachman, Patricia A. Tun, and Christopher B. Rosnick, "Fluid Cognitive Ability Is Associated with Greater Exposure and Smaller Emotional Reactions to Daily Stressors," *Psychology and Aging* 25, no. 2 (2010): 330–42, https://doi.org/10.1037/a0018246 and Paula G. Williams, Yana Suchy, and Holly K. Rau, "Individual Differences in Executive Functioning: Implications for Stress Regulation," *Annals of Behavioral Medicine* 37, no. 2 (2009): 126–40, https://doi.org/10.1007/s12160-009-9100-0.

9. Daniel Maroti, Peter Molander, and Indre Bileviciute-Ljungar, "Differences in Alexithymia and Emotional Awareness in Exhaustion Syndrome and Chronic Fatigue Syndrome," *Scandinavian Journal of Psychology* 58, no. 1 (February 2017): 52–61, doi:10.1111/sjop.12332.

10. Monika H. Donker, Marja C. Erisman, Tamara van Gog, and Tim Mainhard, "Teachers' Emotional Exhaustion: Associations With Their Typical Use of and Implicit Attitudes Toward Emotion Regulation Strategies," *Frontiers in Psychology* 11 (2020): 867, https://doi.org/10.3389/fpsyg.2020.00867 and Christian Grillon, David Quispe-Escudero, Ambika Mathur, and Monique Ernst,

"Mental Fatigue Impairs Emotion Regulation." *Emotion* 15, no. 3 (2015): 383–89, doi:10.1037/emo0000058.

11. Maslach, Schaufeli, and Leiter, "Job Burnout," 399.

12. Maslach, Schaufeli, and Leiter, "Job Burnout," 399.

13. Emer Ryan, Kevin Hore, Jessica Power, and Tracy Jackson, "The Relationship between Physician Burnout and Depression, Anxiety, Suicidality and Substance Abuse: A Mixed Methods Systematic Review," *Frontiers in Public Health* 11 (2023): 1133484, https://doi.org/10.3389/fpubh.2023.1133484.

Chapter 3: Getting Your Life Back Physically

1. "Edsel Ford Dies in Detroit at 49," *New York Times*, May 26, 1943.

2. "Ford Raises Pay of 28,000," *New York Times*, January 2, 1919.

3. Richard Bak, *Henry and Edsel: The Creation of the Ford Empire* (Hoboken, NJ: Wiley, 2003). This is an excellent resource on the story of the challenging and often tense relationship between Edsel and Henry Ford.

4. Steven Watts, *The People's Tycoon: Henry Ford and the American Century*, 1st ed. (New York: Alfred A. Knopf, 2005), 360.

5. Watts, *The People's Tycoon*, chapter 18.

6. Bak, *Henry and Edsel*, 228–29.

7. Watts, *The People's Tycoon*.

8. Bak, *Henry and Edsel*, 258.

9. Paul Bennett, "Gastric and Duodenal Ulcers," in *Cambridge Handbook of Psychology, Health and Medicine*, ed. Susan Ayers, Andrew Baum, Chris McManus, et al., 2nd ed. (Cambridge: Cambridge University Press, 2007); Jerrold S. Greenberg, *Comprehensive Stress Management*, 14th ed. (New York: McGraw Hill, 2017), 53; Susan Levenstein, "The Very Model of a Modern Etiology: A Biopsychosocial View of Peptic Ulcer," *Psychosomatic Medicine* 62, no. 2 (2000): 176–85, https://doi.org/10.1097/00006842-200003000-00003; and Yoichi Chida, Mark Hamer, Jane Wardle, and Andrew Steptoe, "Do Stress-Related Psychosocial Factors Contribute to Cancer Incidence and Survival?" *Nature Clinical Practice Oncology* 5, 8 (2008): 466–75, doi:https://doi.org/10.1038/ncponc1134.

10. Hanumanthappa Pradeep, Joseph B. Diya, Shivaiah Shashikumar, and Golgodu K. Rajanikant, "Oxidative Stress—Assassin behind the Ischemic Stroke," *Folia Neuropathologica* 50, no. 3 (2012): 219–30, https://doi.org/10.5114/fn.2012.30522.

11. Ronald Glaser, Janice K. Kiecolt-Glaser, *Handbook of Human Stress and Immunity*, (Amsterdam: Elsevier Science, 2014). This is a substantial text, and it's the best starting point for anyone wanting to delve deeply into the research about stress and immune system function.

12. Nicolas Rohleder, "Chronic Stress and Disease," in *Insights to Neuroimmune Biology* (Amsterdam: Elsevier Inc, 2016), 207–08.

13. Selye, *The Stress of Life*, 36.

14. Lovallo, *Stress and Health*. The most complete and straightforward explanation of the stress response I've seen is in Dr. Lovallo's excellent text.

15. J. Wardle and E. L. Gibson, "Diet and Stress: Interactions with Emotions and Behavior," in *Stress: Concepts, Cognition, Emotion, and Behavior* (Amsterdam: Elsevier Inc, 2016), 435–43.

16. Wardle and Gibson, "Diet and Stress," 439–40.

17. Wardle and Gibson, "Diet and Stress," 440.

18. Michael D. Wirth, Nitin Shivappa, James B. Burch, Thomas G. Hurley, and James R. Hébert, "The Dietary Inflammatory Index, Shift Work, and Depression: Results from NHANES," *Health Psychology* 36, no. 8 (2017): 760–69. doi:10.1037/hea0000514.

19. Catherine Itsiopoulos, Hannah L. Mayr, and Colleen J. Thomas, "The Anti-Inflammatory Effects of a Mediterranean Diet: A Review," *Current Opinion in Clinical Nutrition and Metabolic Care*, 25, no. 6 (2022): 415–22. https://doi.org/10.1097/MCO.0000000000000872.

20. Achim Elfering, Maria U. Kottwitz, Özgür Tamcan, Urs Müller, and Anne F. Mannion, "Impaired Sleep Predicts Onset of Low Back Pain and Burnout Symptoms: Evidence from a Three-Wave Study," *Psychology, Health & Medicine* 23, no. 10 (2018): 1196–1210 and Amanda Ritsma and Lauren Forrest, "Causes of Chronic Stress and Impact on Physician Health," in *Humanism and Resilience in Residency Training* (Cham, Switzerland: Springer, 2020), 257.

21. Lovallo, Stress and Health, 76.

22. Anand Thirupathi, Meizi Wang, Ji Kai Lin, Gusztáv Fekete, Bíró István, Julien S. Baker, and Yaodong Gu, "Effect of Different Exercise Modalities on Oxidative Stress: A Systematic Review," *BioMed Research International* (2021): 1947928–10. https://doi.org/10.1155/2021/1947928.

23. Yael Netz, "Is the Comparison between Exercise and Pharmacologic Treatment of Depression in the Clinical Practice Guideline of the American College of Physicians Evidence-Based?" *Frontiers in Pharmacology* 8, (2017): 257.

Chapter 4: Getting Your Life Back Emotionally

1. Peter Rader, *Mike Wallace: A Life* (New York: Thomas Dunne Books, 2012) 207.

2. Adam Bernstein, "Mike Wallace Dies; Veteran Journalist and Former '60 Minutes' Correspondent was 93," *The Washington Post*, April 8, 2012, accessed Feb 28, 2024, https://www.washingtonpost.com/local/obituaries/mike-wallace-dies-veteran-journalist-and-former-60-minutes-interviewer-was-93/2012/04/08/gIQAwzIu3S_story.html.

3. Rader, *Mike Wallace: A Life*, chapters 21 and 22.

4. Mike Wallace, "Guideposts Classics: Mike Wallace on Coping with Depression," accessed Feb 28, 2024, https://guideposts.org/positive-living/health-and-wellness/coping-with-illness/guideposts-classics-mike-wallace-on-coping-with-depression/.

5. Mike Wallace, Mary Wallace, and Eric Kandel, interview by Jeffrey Borenstein, "Healthy Minds—Depression Featuring a Conversation with Mike Wallace," *Healthy Minds with Dr. Jeffrey Borenstein*, November 24, 2008, Brainline.org, accessed August 30, 2023, https://www.brainline.org/sites/default /files/video/transcript/healthy_minds_depression.pdf, 2.

6. Rader, *Mike Wallace: A Life*, 207, 227.

7. Wallace, "Guideposts Classics: Mike Wallace on Coping with Depression." Notice in this *Guideposts* article that Mike Wallace himself chooses to quote a CBS official saying that he was admitted to the hospital "suffering from exhaustion" rather than characterize the episode as a suicide attempt, which he would only do later in life, as seen in the interview with Jeffrey Borenstein, "Healthy Minds—Depression Featuring a Conversation with Mike Wallace."

8. David Balayssac, Bruno Pereira, Julie Virot, Aurore Collin, David Alapini, Damien Cuny, Jean-Marc Gagnaire, Nicolas Authier, and Brigitte Vennat, "Burnout, Associated Comorbidities and Coping Strategies in French Community Pharmacies—BOP Study: A Nationwide Cross-Sectional Study." *PloS One* 12, no. 8 (2017): e0182956–e0182956, https://doi.org/10.1371/journal .pone.0182956 and Dela M. van Dijk, Willem van Rhenen, Jaap M. J. Murre, and Esmée Verwijk, "Cognitive Functioning, Sleep Quality, and Work Performance in Non-Clinical Burnout: The Role of Working Memory," *PloS One* 15, no. 4 (2020): e0231906–e0231906, https://doi.org/10.1371/journal.pone .0231906.

9. Neal Gabler, *Walt Disney* (New York: Knopf Doubleday Publishing Group, 2006), 164.

10. F. S. Fitzgerald, *The Crack-Up* (London: Alma Books, 2018).

11. "Chaplin Says Wife Can't Realize Suit," *New York Times*, January 23, 1927, accessed August 30, 2023, https://timesmachine.nytimes.com/timesmachine /1927/01/23/97135811.html?pageNumber=12.

12. Belmiro Freitas de Salles, Roberto Simão, Fabrício Miranda, Jefferson da Silva Novaes, Adriana Lemos, and Jeffrey M. Willardson, "Rest Interval between Sets in Strength Training," *Sports Medicine (Auckland)* 39, no. 9 (2009): 765–77, https://doi.org/10.2165/11315230-000000000-00000.

13. Freitas de Salles et al., "Rest Interval between Sets in Strength Training," 765–77.

14. M. S. Hallbeck, B. R. Lowndes, J. Bingener, A. M. Abdelrahman, D. Yu, A. Bartley, and A. E. Park, "The Impact of Intraoperative Microbreaks with Exercises on Surgeons: A Multi-Center Cohort Study," *Applied Ergonomics* 60, (April 1, 2017): 334–41, https://dx.doi.org/10.1016/j.apergo.2016.12.006.

15. Jerrold S. Greenberg, *Comprehensive Stress Management*, 14th ed. (New York: McGraw Hill, 2017), part 3.

16. Lovallo, *Stress and Health*, chapter 3.

17. Kenneth S. Wuest, *Wuest's Word Studies from the Greek New Testament for the English Reader*, vol. 1. (Grand Rapids, MI: Eerdmans, 1997), 132.

Chapter 5: Getting Your Life Back Relationally

1. Mia Pihlaja, Jari Peräkylä, Emma-Helka Erkkilä, Emilia Tapio, Maiju Vertanen, and Kaisa M. Hartikainen, "Altered Neural Processes Underlying Executive Function in Occupational Burnout—Basis for a Novel EEG Biomarker," *Frontiers in Human Neuroscience* 17 (2023): 1194714–1194714, https://doi.org/10.3389/fnhum.2023.1194714.

2. Maslach, Schaufeli, and Leiter, "Job Burnout," 399.

3. Jonathan Hoover, "Can Christians Practice Mindfulness without Compromising Their Values?" *Journal of Psychology and Christianity* 37, no. 3 (2018): 247–55.

4. Stevan E. Hobfoll and John Freedy, "Conservation of Resources: A General Stress Theory Applied to Burnout," in *Professional Burnout*, ed. Wilmar B. Schaufeli, Christina Maslach, and Tadeusz Marek (New York: Routledge, 2018), 115–129.

5. W. E. Vine, Merrill F. Unger, and William White Jr., *Vine's Complete Expository Dictionary of Old and New Testament Words*, vol. 2. (Nashville: Thomas Nelson, 1996).

6. Archibald Thomas Robertson, *Word Pictures in the New Testament* (Nashville: Broadman Press, 1933) and Horst Robert Balz and Gerhard Schneider, eds. *Exegetical Dictionary of the New Testament*, vol. 2. (Grand Rapids, MI: Eerdmans. 1990).

Chapter 6: Getting Your Life Back Spiritually

1. I'm not suggesting that using bad language is an indicator of not being a child of God; my point is that my dad modeled exemplary spiritual self-discipline as I was growing up.

2. John F. MacArthur Jr., *MacArthur New Testament Commentary: John 1–11* (Chicago: Moody Press, 2006).

3. MacArthur, *MacArthur New Testament Commentary: John 1–11*.

4. Etienne Koechlin, "Prefrontal Executive Function and Adaptive Behavior in Complex Environments," *Current Opinion in Neurobiology* 37 (2016): 1–6, https://doi.org/10.1016/j.conb.2015.11.004.

5. Robert G. Bratcher and William D. Reyburn, *A Translator's Handbook on the Book of Psalms* (New York: United Bible Societies, 1991), 740.

6. Walter A. Elwell and Philip W. Comfort, eds., *Tyndale Bible Dictionary* (Wheaton, IL: Tyndale House Publishers, 2001), 140.

7. Allen C. Myers, ed., *The Eerdmans Bible Dictionary* (Grand Rapids, MI: Eerdmans, 1987).

Chapter 7: Getting Your Life Back Occupationally

1. Hanna M. Gavelin, Magdalena E. Domellöf, Elisabeth Åström, Andreas Nelson, Nathalie H. Launder, Anna Stigsdotter Neely, and Amit Lampit, "Cognitive Function in Clinical Burnout: A Systematic Review and Meta-Analysis,"

Work & Stress 36, no. 1 (January 2022): 86–104. doi:10.1080/02678373.2021.20 02972.

2. Dimitri Van Der Linden, Ger P.J. Keijsers, Paul Eling, and Rachel Van Schaijk, "Work Stress and Attentional Difficulties: An Initial Study on Burnout and Cognitive Failures," *Work and Stress* 19, no. 1 (2005): 23–36, https://doi.org/10.1080/02678370500065275. This source explains how "lapses" of attention are more common with burnout and gives a potential explanation.

3. This occurs because of a chain reaction; as we'll see, burnout is associated with reduced executive function, and reduced executive function is associated with creativity deficits: Darya L. Zabelina, Naomi P. Friedman, and Jessica Andrews-Hanna, "Unity and Diversity of Executive Functions in Creativity," *Consciousness and Cognition* 68 (2019): 47–56, https://doi.org/10.1016/j.concog.2018.12.005.

4. This is another facet of the reduced executive control (or executive function) associated with burnout. Damasio gives a great explanation of the social implications of reduced activity in the prefrontal cortex: Antonio R. Damasio, "On Some Functions of the Human Prefrontal Cortex," *Annals of the New York Academy of Sciences* 769, no. 1 (1995): 241–52, https://doi.org/10.1111/j.1749-6632.1995.tb38142.x.

5. David B. Arciniegas, C. Alan Anderson, and Christopher M. Filley, "Executive Function," in *Behavioral Neurology and Neuropsychiatry* (United Kingdom: Cambridge University Press, 2013).

6. Arnsten, "Stress Signalling Pathways That Impair Prefrontal Cortex Structure and Function," 410–22.

7. Johannes Beck, Markus Gerber, Serge Brand, Uwe Pühse, and Edith Holsboer-Trachsler, "Executive Function Performance Is Reduced during Occupational Burnout but Can Recover to the Level of Healthy Controls," *Journal of Psychiatric Research* 47, no. 11 (2013): 1824–30, https://doi.org/10.1016/j.jpsychires.2013.08.009.

8. Bak, *Henry and Edsel*, 133.

9. Warren K. Bickel, David P. Jarmolowicz, E. Terry Mueller, Kirstin M. Gatchalian, and Samuel M. McClure, "Are Executive Function and Impulsivity Antipodes? A Conceptual Reconstruction with Special Reference to Addiction," *Psychopharmacologia* 221, no. 3 (2012): 361–87, https://doi.org/10.1007/s00213-012-2689-x.

10. Pavlos Deligkaris, Efharis Panagopoulou, Anthony J. Montgomery, and Elvira Masoura, "Job Burnout and Cognitive Functioning: A Systematic Review," *Work and Stress* 28, no. 2 (2014): 107–23, https://doi.org/10.1080/02678373.2014.909545, p. 117.

11. Dorit Ben Shalom, "The Amygdala–Insula–Medial Prefrontal Cortex–Lateral Prefrontal Cortex Pathway and Its Disorders," *Frontiers in Neuroanatomy* 16 (2022): 1028546–1028546, https://doi.org/103389/fnana.2022.1028546.

12. Maria Ironside, Michael Browning, Tahereh L. Ansari, Christopher J. Harvey, Mama N. Sekyi-Djan, Sonia J. Bishop, Catherine J. Harmer, and Jacinta O'Shea, "Effect of Prefrontal Cortex Stimulation on Regulation of Amygdala

Response to Threat in Individuals with Trait Anxiety: A Randomized Clinical Trial," *Archives of General Psychiatry* 76, no. 1 (2019): 71–78, https://doi.org/10.1001/jamapsychiatry.2018.2172.

13. Joseph E. LeDoux, "Emotion Circuits in the Brain," *Annual Review of Neuroscience* 7, no. 2 (2000): 274, https://doi.org/10.1176/foc.7.2.foc274.

BIBLIOGRAPHY

These resources offer additional support for the conclusions in the text and provide the reader with a sampling of sources for study in different categories.

Chapter 1: Nietzsche or Goldilocks?

Eustress and Distress

Selye, Hans. *The Stress of Life*. 2nd ed. New York: McGraw-Hill, 1978.

Bell Curve of Stress

Arnsten, Amy F. T. "Stress Signalling Pathways that Impair Prefrontal Cortex Structure and Function." *Nature Reviews Neuroscience* 10, no. 6 (2009): 410–422. https://doi.org/10.1038/nrn2648.

Dolan, Simon L. *De-Stress at Work: Understanding and Combatting Chronic Stress*. Vol. 1. United Kingdom: Routledge, 2023.

Ritsma, Amanda, and Lauren Forrest. "Causes of Chronic Stress and Impact on Physician Health." In *Humanism and Resilience in Residency Training*, 247–271. Cham, Switzerland: Springer Nature, 2020.

Physiological Response to Stress

Lovallo, William R. *Stress and Health: Biological and Psychological Interactions*. 3rd ed. Los Angeles, CA: SAGE Publications, Inc, 2016.
   Note: there are many wonderful resources that deal with this very complex topic. Dr. Lovallo's text is my favorite source, and it's a great starting place if you wish to learn more about the way our bodies respond to stress.

Overreaching and Overtraining

Lovallo, William R. *Stress and Health: Biological and Psychological Interactions.* 3rd ed. Los Angeles, CA: SAGE Publications, Inc, 2016.

Meeusen, Romain. "The Overtraining Syndrome: Diagnosis and Management." In *The Olympic Textbook of Medicine in Sport*, 138–159. Oxford, UK: Wiley-Blackwell, 2008.

Chapter 2: Super Rats

Dr. Selye's "Super Rats" Experiment

Selye, H. *The Stress of Life.* 2nd ed. New York: McGraw-Hill, 1978, 112–13.

The "General Adaptation Syndrome" (Alarm, Adaptation, Exhaustion)

Selye, H. *The Stress of Life.* 2nd ed. New York: McGraw-Hill, 1978.

Dr. Christina Maslach's Model of Burnout

Maslach, C. "Burnout: A Multidimensional Perspective." In *Professional Burnout*, edited by Wilmar B. Schaufeli, Christina Maslach, and Tadeusz Marek. 1st ed., 19–32. New York: Routledge, 2018.

Maslach, C., and Michael P. Leiter. "Understanding Burnout." In *The Handbook of Stress and Health: A Guide to Research and Practice*, edited by Cary L. Cooper and James C. Quick. Oxford: Wiley, 2017.

Maslach, C., and Wilmar B. Schaufeli. "Historical and Conceptual Development of Burnout." In *Professional Burnout*, edited by Wilmar B. Schaufeli, Christina Maslach, and Tadeusz Marek. 1st ed., 1–16. New York: Routledge, 2018.

Chapter 3: Getting Your Life Back Physically

Edsel Ford's Relationship with His Father and His Early Demise

Bak, Richard. *Henry and Edsel: The Creation of the Ford Empire.* Hoboken, NJ: Wiley, 2003.

Watts, Steven. *The People's Tycoon: Henry Ford and the American Century.* 1st ed. New York: Alfred A. Knopf, 2005.

Chronic Stress and Your Body: Chronic Stress Can Cause You to Have Cardiovascular Problems

Greenberg, Jerrold. *Comprehensive Stress Management.* New York: McGraw-Hill US Higher Ed ISE, 2020.

Lovallo, William R. *Stress and Health: Biological and Psychological Interactions.* 3rd ed. Los Angeles, CA: SAGE Publications, Inc, 2016.

Chronic Stress Can Impact the Immune System

Lovallo, William R. *Stress and Health: Biological and Psychological Interactions.* 3rd ed. Los Angeles, CA: SAGE Publications, Inc, 2016.

Manigault, Andrew W., and Peggy M. Zoccola. "Psychoneuroimmunology: How Chronic Stress Makes Us Sick." In *Biopsychosocial Factors of Stress, and Mindfulness for Stress Reduction,* edited by H. Hazlett-Stevens, 83–103. Cham, Switzerland: Springer Nature, 2022.

Rohleder, Nicolas. "Chronic Stress and Disease." In *Insights to Neuroimmune Biology,* 201–14. Amsterdam: Elsevier Inc, 2016.

Rohleder, Nicolas. "Stress and Inflammation—the Need to Address the Gap in the Transition between Acute and Chronic Stress Effects." *Psychoneuroendocrinology: Psychoneuroendocrinology* 105, (2019): 164–171.

Schneiderman, Laura, and Andrew Baum. "Acute and Chronic Stress and the Immune System." In *Stress and Disease Processes* 1st ed., 1–25. United Kingdom: Routledge, 1992.

Chronic Stress Can Contribute to Bodily Inflammation

Manigault, Andrew W., and Peggy M. Zoccola. "Psychoneuroimmunology: How Chronic Stress Makes Us Sick." In *Biopsychosocial Factors of Stress, and Mindfulness for Stress Reduction,* edited by H. Hazlett-Stevens, 83–103. Cham, Switzerland: Springer Nature, 2022.

Rohleder, Nicolas. "Chronic Stress and Disease." In *Insights to Neuroimmune Biology,* 201–14. Amsterdam: Elsevier Inc, 2016.

Rohleder, Nicolas. "Stress and Inflammation—the Need to Address the Gap in the Transition between Acute and Chronic Stress Effects." *Psychoneuroendocrinology* 105, (2019): 164–171.

Chronic Stress Can Cause Bodily Pain and Muscle Tension

Dolan, Simon L. *De-Stress at Work: Understanding and Combatting Chronic Stress.* Vol. 1. United Kingdom: Routledge, 2023.

Greenberg, Jerrold. *Comprehensive Stress Management.* New York: McGraw-Hill US Higher Ed ISE, 2020.

Stress Is a Generalized Response

Lovallo, William R. *Stress and Health: Biological and Psychological Interactions.* 3rd ed. Los Angeles, CA: SAGE Publications, Inc, 2016.

Selye, H. *The Stress of Life.* 2nd ed. New York: McGraw-Hill, 1978, page 55.

The Body's Stress Response

Greenberg, Jerrold. *Comprehensive Stress Management.* New York: McGraw-Hill US Higher Ed ISE, 2020.

Lovallo, William R. *Stress and Health: Biological and Psychological Interactions.* 3rd ed. Los Angeles, CA: SAGE Publications, Inc, 2016.

Diet and Stress

Wardle, J., and E. L. Gibson. "Diet and Stress: Interactions with Emotions and Behavior." In *Stress: Concepts, Cognition, Emotion, and Behavior*, 435–43: Amsterdam: Elsevier Inc, 2016.

Sleep and Burnout/Chronic Stress

Elfering, Achim, Maria U. Kottwitz, Özgür Tamcan, Urs Müller, and Anne F. Mannion. "Impaired Sleep Predicts Onset of Low Back Pain and Burnout Symptoms: Evidence from a Three-Wave Study." *Psychology, Health & Medicine* 23, no. 10 (2018): 1196–1210.

Grossi, Giorgio, Aleksander Perski, Walter Osika, and Ivanka Savic. "Stress-Related Exhaustion Disorder—Clinical Manifestation of Burnout? A Review of Assessment Methods, Sleep Impairments, Cognitive Disturbances, and Neuro-Biological and Physiological Changes in Clinical Burnout." *Scandinavian Journal of Psychology* 56, no. 6 (2015): 626–36.

Hemmeter, Ulrich-Michael. "Treatment of Burnout: Overlap of Diagnosis." In *Burnout for Experts*, 73–87. Boston, MA: Springer US, 2013.

Sørengaard, Torhild Anita, and Ingvild Saksvik-Lehouillier. "Associations between Burnout Symptoms and Sleep among Workers during the COVID-19 Pandemic." *Sleep Medicine* 90 (2022): 199–203. doi:10.1016/j.sleep.2022.01.022.

Sleep Hygiene

Hauri, Peter J. "Sleep/Wake Lifestyle Modifications: Sleep Hygiene." In *Therapy in Sleep Medicine*, 151–60, 2012. https://doi.org/10.1016/B978-1-4377-1703-7.10011-8.

Murray, Susan L., and Matthew S. Thimgan. "Sleep Hygiene Recommendations." In *Human Fatigue Risk Management*. United States: Elsevier Science & Technology, 2016.

Exercise and the Stress Response

Greenberg, Jerrold. *Comprehensive Stress Management*. New York: McGraw-Hill US Higher Ed ISE, 2020.

Lovallo, William R. *Stress and Health: Biological and Psychological Interactions*. 3rd ed. Los Angeles, CA: SAGE Publications, Inc, 2016.

Exercise Effectiveness Compared with Antidepressants

Netz, Yael. "Is the Comparison between Exercise and Pharmacologic Treatment of Depression in the Clinical Practice Guideline of the American College of Physicians Evidence-Based?" *Frontiers in Pharmacology* 8, (2017): 257.

Chapter 4: Getting Your Life Back Emotionally

Mike Wallace Story

Rader, Peter. *Mike Wallace: A Life*. 1st ed. New York: Thomas Dunne Books, 2012.

Wallace, Mike. "Guideposts Classics: Mike Wallace on Coping with Depression." https://guideposts.org/positive-living/health-and-wellness/coping-with-illness/guideposts-classics-mike-wallace-on-coping-with-depression/

Wallace, Mike, Mary Wallace, and Eric Kandel, interview by Jeffrey Borenstein. "Healthy Minds—Depression Featuring a Conversation with Mike Wallace." *Healthy Minds with Dr. Jeffrey Borenstein*, November 24, 2008, Brainline.org, https://www.brainline.org/sites/default/files/video/transcript/healthy_minds_depression.pdf.

Weiner, Tim. "Mike Wallace, CBS Pioneer of '60 Minutes,' Dies at 93." https://www.nytimes.com/2012/04/09/business/media/mike-wallace-cbs-pioneer-of-60-minutes-dead-at-93.html.

Walt Disney's "Emotional Flap" Comment

Gabler, Neal. *Walt Disney.* New York: Knopf Doubleday Publishing Group, 2006, 164.

F. Scott Fitzgerald's "Crack-Up"

Fitzgerald, F. S. *The Crack-Up.* London: Alma Books, 2018.

Charlie Chaplin's Apparent Suicide Attempt

"Chaplin Says Wife Can't Realize Suit." *New York Times*, January 23, 1927, https://timesmachine.nytimes.com/timesmachine/1927/01/23/97135811.html?pageNumber=12 (accessed August 30, 2023).

Rest Intervals Are Important in the Area of Physical Exercise

Freitas de Salles, Belmiro, Roberto Simao, Fabricio Miranda, Jefferson da Silva Novaes, Adriana Lemos, and Jeffrey M. Willardson. "Rest Interval between Sets in Strength Training." *Sports Medicine (Auckland)* 39, no. 9 (January 1, 2009): 765–77, https://doi.org/10.2165/11315230-000000000-00000.

Surgeons Using Microbreaks

Hallbeck, M. S., B. R. Lowndes, J. Bingener, A. M. Abdelrahman, D. Yu, A. Bartley, and A. E. Park. "The Impact of Intraoperative Microbreaks with Exercises on Surgeons: A Multi-Center Cohort Study." *Applied Ergonomics* 60, (April 1, 2017): 334–341, https://dx.doi.org/10.1016/j.apergo.2016.12.006.

Relaxation Techniques

Greenberg, Jerrold. *Comprehensive Stress Management.* New York: McGraw-Hill US Higher Ed ISE, 2020.

Some Examples of Christian Accommodative Mindfulness

Ford, Kristy, and Fernando Garzon. "Research Note: A Randomized Investigation of Evangelical Christian Accommodative Mindfulness." *Spirituality in Clinical Practice (Washington, DC)* 4, no. 2 (2017): 92–99.

Garzon, Fernando, and Kristy Ford. "Adapting Mindfulness for Conservative Christians." *The Journal of Psychology and Christianity* 35, no. 3 (2016): 263.

Emotional Intelligence and Burnout

Moon, Tae Won, and Won-Moo Hur. "Emotional Intelligence, Emotional Exhaustion, and Job Performance." *Social Behavior and Personality* 39, no. 8 (September 1, 2011): 1087–96, https://www.ingentaconnect.com/content/sbp/sbp/2011/00000039/00000008/art00008.

Weng, Hui-Ching, Chao-Ming Hung, Yi-Tien Liu, Yu-Jen Cheng, Cheng-Yo Yen, Chi-Chang Chang, and Chih-Kun Huang. "Associations between Emotional Intelligence and Doctor Burnout, Job Satisfaction and Patient Satisfaction." *Medical Education* 45, no. 8 (2011): 835–42. doi:10.1111/j.1365-2923.2011.03985.x.

Stress and the Brain Structures

Arnsten, Amy F. T. "Stress Signalling Pathways that Impair Prefrontal Cortex Structure and Function." *Nature Reviews Neuroscience* 10, no. 6 (2009): 410–422.

Kleshchova, Olena, and Mariann R. Weierich. "The Neurobiology of Stress." In *Biopsychosocial Factors of Stress, and Mindfulness for Stress Reduction*, edited by H. Hazlett-Stevens, 17–65. Cham, Switzerland: Springer, 2022.

Lovallo, William R. *Stress and Health: Biological and Psychological Interactions.* 3rd ed. Los Angeles, CA: SAGE Publications, Inc, 2016.

Lupien, Sonia J., Robert-Paul Juster, Catherine Raymond, and Marie-France Marin. "The Effects of Chronic Stress on the Human Brain: From Neurotoxicity, to Vulnerability, to Opportunity." *Frontiers in Neuroendocrinology* 49, (2018): 91–105.

Smith, Rebecca P., Craig L. Katz, Dennis S. Charney, and Steven M. Southwick. "Neurobiology of Disaster Exposure: Fear, Anxiety, Trauma, and Resilience." In *Textbook of Disaster Psychiatry*, edited by Robert J. Ursano et al., 97–118. Cambridge: Cambridge University Press, 2007, http://dx.doi.org/10.1017/CBO9780511544415.006.

Thiel, Kenneth J., and Michael N. Dretsch. "The Basics of the Stress Response." *The Handbook of Stress: Neuropsychological Effects on the Brain*, edited by Cheryl D. Conrad, 67–101. United Kingdom: Blackwell Publishing, 2011.

Wellman, Cara L. "Chronic Stress Effects on Corticolimbic Morphology." *The Handbook of Stress: Neuropsychological Effects on the Brain*, edited by Cheryl D. Conrad, 201–229. United Kingdom: Blackwell Publishing, 2011.

Mindfulness as a Healthy Practice that Christians Can Use

Hoover, Jonathan. "Can Christians Practice Mindfulness without Compromising their Values?" *Journal of Psychology and Christianity* 37, no. 3 (2018): 247–255.

Chapter 5: Getting Your Life Back Relationally

Emotional Intelligence and Burnout

Zeidner, Moshe, Gerald Matthews, and Richard D. Roberts. "How Social Is Emotional Intelligence?" In *What We Know about Emotional Intelligence*, 169–202. Cambridge, Massachusetts: The MIT Press, 2009. https://doi.org /10.7551/mitpress/7404.003.0012.

Chapter 7: Getting Your Life Back Occupationally

Executive Functions of the Brain and How They Are Impacted by Stress (key to Dr. Hoover's conceptualization of "Burnout Brain")

Ardila, Alfredo. "Executive Functions Brain Functional System." In *Dysexecutive Syndromes*, edited by Alfredo Ardila, Shameem Fatima, and Mónica Rosselli, 29–41. Switzerland: Springer International Publishing AG, 2019, https://link.springer.com/chapter/10.1007/978-3-030-25077-5_2.

Gavelin, Hanna M., Magdalena E. Domellöf, Elisabeth Åström, Andreas Nelson, Nathalie H. Launder, Anna Stigsdotter Neely, and Amit Lampit. "Cognitive Function in Clinical Burnout: A Systematic Review and Meta-Analysis." *Work & Stress* 36, no. 1 (2021): 86–104. https://dx.doi.org/10.1080 /02678373.2021.2002972.

Girotti, Milena, Samantha M. Adler, Sarah E. Bulin, Elizabeth A. Fucich, Denisse Paredes, and David A. Morilak. "Prefrontal Cortex Executive Processes Affected by Stress in Health and Disease." *Progress in Neuro-Psychopharmacology and Biological Psychiatry* 85, (July 13, 2018): 161–179, https://dx.doi.org/10.1016/j.pnpbp.2017.07.004.

Hersh, Matthew A. "How's Your Frontal Lobe Doing? and Other Executive Functioning Questions." In *The Thriving Therapist: Sustainable Self-Care to Prevent Burnout and Enhance Well-Being*, edited by M. A. Hersh, 145–51. Washington, DC: American Psychological Association, 2022.

Kleshchova, Olena, and Mariann R. Weierich. "The Neurobiology of Stress." In *Biopsychosocial Factors of Stress, and Mindfulness for Stress Reduction*, edited by H. Hazlett-Stevens, 17–65. Cham, Switzerland: Springer, 2022.

Lovallo, William R. *Stress and Health: Biological and Psychological Interactions*. 3rd ed. Los Angeles, CA: SAGE Publications, Inc, 2016.

Lupien, Sonia J., Robert-Paul Juster, Catherine Raymond, and Marie-France Marin. "The Effects of Chronic Stress on the Human Brain: From Neurotoxicity, to Vulnerability, to Opportunity." *Frontiers in Neuroendocrinology* 49, (2018): 91–105.

Wolff, Max, Sören Enge, Anja Kräplin, Klaus-martin Krönke, Gerhard Bühringer, Michael N. Smolka, and Thomas Goschke. "Chronic Stress, Executive Functioning, and Real-life Self-control: An Experience Sampling Study." *Journal of Personality* 89, no. 3 (2021): 402–21. doi:10.1111/jopy.12587.

Prefrontal Cortex

Fuster, Joaquin. *The Prefrontal Cortex.* 5th ed. Burlington: Elsevier Science, 2015, figure 2.2.

Henry Ford Rips Apart a New Car

Watts, Steven. *The People's Tycoon: Henry Ford and the American Century.* 1st ed. New York: Alfred A. Knopf, 2005.

The Amygdala and Prefrontal Cortex During Stress

Lovallo, William R. *Stress and Health: Biological and Psychological Interactions.* 3rd ed. Los Angeles, CA: SAGE Publications, Inc, 2016.

Smith, Rebecca P., Craig L. Katz, Dennis S. Charney, and Steven M. Southwick. "Neurobiology of Disaster Exposure: Fear, Anxiety, Trauma, and Resilience." In *Textbook of Disaster Psychiatry*, 97–118. Cambridge: Cambridge University Press, 2007. http://dx.doi.org/10.1017/CBO9780511544415.006.

DR. JONATHAN HOOVER is the senior associate pastor at NewSpring Church in Wichita, Kansas, and the program director of the master of science in general psychology program at Regent University in Virginia Beach, Virginia. As a communicator, Jonathan is known for his ability to integrate psychological science and Christian belief in an easy-to-understand way. Jonathan is a researcher in the field  of psychology and is now actively researching burnout. Jonathan has been married to his wife, Wendy, since 2002, and they have been greatly blessed with two amazing daughters, Cheyenne and Summer.